Sephardi Religious Responses to Modernity

The Sherman Lecture Series

The Sherman Lecture Series is an annual series supported by the Sherman Trust on behalf of the School of Oriental and African Studies, London, UK.

Edited by Dr Tudor Parfitt and Professor John Hinnels, School of Oriental and African Studies, London, UK.

Volume 1 *Sephardi Religious Responses to Modernity*
Norman A. Stillman

Other volumes in preparation

Volume 2 *The Interaction of Religion and Politics: The Case of Israel*
Charles S. Liebmann

ISSN 1023-7917

This book is part of a series. The publisher will accept continuation orders which may be cancelled at any time and which provide for automatic billing and shipping of each title upon publication. Please write for details.

Sephardi Religious Responses to Modernity

Norman A. Stillman
University of Oklahoma
USA

harwood academic publishers
Australia • Austria • China • France • Germany • India • Japan
Luxembourg • Malaysia • Netherlands • Russia • Singapore
Switzerland • Thailand • United Kingdom • United States

3 Boulevard Royal
L-2449 Luxembourg

British Library Cataloguing in Publication Data

Stillman, Norman A.
Sephardi Religious Responses to
Modernity. — (Sherman Lecture Series,
ISSN 1023-7917; Vol. 1)
I. Title   II. Series
296.8

ISBN 3-7186-5699-X

Front Cover
Rabbi Ovadia Yosef in a moment of meditation (Photograph by Joel Fishman)

To our dear Jennie

Who has immeasurably enriched our family's life with her love and friendship

Contents

Plates

Acknowledgements

Gratitude may be, in the words of Robert Louis Stevenson, "a lame sentiment," but its expression is a duty, and a pleasurable one at that. I am deeply grateful to the many individuals and institutions connected with the writing and publication of this book which is based upon my Sherman Lectures delivered at the School of Oriental and African Studies of the University of London, from 28 February to 3 March 1994.

My warmest thanks to Dr Tudor Parfitt, Director of the Centre for Jewish Studies at S.O.A.S. for having initially suggested my name to Professor John R. Hinnells, the Head of the Department of the Study of Religions at S.O.A.S. and the administrator of the lecture series. And of course, my thanks to Professor Hinnells for having invited me. Both he and Dr Parfitt were the most gracious and cordial of hosts. Naturally, thanks are due to the Sherman Trust for endowing the lectures. I was deeply honored to have been chosen to inaugurate the series.

My stay in London was kindly facilitated by Mr E.D. Ishag, who very generously provided me with comfortable accommodation. I have Mr Sidney L. Shipton of the Ta'ali World Movement for a United Israel to thank for having made the initial contact with Mr Ishag. Dr Max Levene showed me many personal kindnesses while I was in London and contributed to making my stay there a pleasant one.

Over the years, my thoughts on the subject of Sephardi and Oriental Jewish religiosity and more particularly on the subject of Sephardi responses to modernity have benefitted greatly from conversations with Professors Menahem Ben-Sasson and Harvey Goldberg of the Hebrew University, Shlomo Deshen and Moshe Shokeid of Tel Aviv University, Dr Zvi Zohar of the Shalom Hartman Institute, and Rabbi Dr Marc D. Angel of the Spanish and Portuguese Congregation Shearith Israel of New York. My profound intellectual debt to a number of them will be obvious from the numerous citations of their works throughout this book.

Zvi Zohar was particularly kind in tracking down and sending me an elusive reference that I needed on the very day he returned home from several weeks of reserve military duty. I regret that his important new book *Tradition and Change: Halachic Responses of Middle Eastern Rabbis to Legal and Technological Change (Egypt and Syria, 1880–1920)* (Jerusalem, 1993) reached me only after my book had gone to press and thus could not be cited in the notes. It is, however, included in the Bibliography.

My colleague at Binghamton University, Professor Allan Arkush kindly read the original manuscript of the lectures and offered many valuable critiques and suggestions. In this and other matters pertaining to Jewish intellectual history, he has helped me to clarify my own thinking with his keen and incisive mind.

My graduate student, Mr Josef W. Meri, has been a tremendous help to me as a research assistant, assiduously tracking down with his mastery of computer skills the far-flung locations of source materials in a variety of languages.

As always, the staff of the Binghamton University Interlibrary Loan Office and its director, James J. Mellone, were most helpful, cheerfully expediting dozens of requests for rare bibliographical items not available to me in Binghamton.

Some of the research that went into this book was conducted as part of a broader research project under a grant from the Maurice Amado Foundation through its Sephardic Education Project. Final editing and seeing the manuscript through the press was done while on sabbatical leave from Binghamton University while in Israel as Lady Davis Fellow at the Hebrew University in Jerusalem and Dayan Fellow at the Dayan Center for Middle Eastern and African Studies at Tel-Aviv University in Ramat Aviv during the academic year 1994–1995.

Finally, it is customary for an author to acknowledge his indebtedness to his family for their loving support and encouragement. My case has always been special. My wife Yedida is my closest colleague. We have collaborated on research projects, books, and articles. Even on independent intellectual ventures, we consult a great deal with one another – and this book is no exception. My acquaintance with various aspects of popular religion discussed in Chapter Four owes much to her. Indeed, it was she who first introduced me to the spirit of Sephardi religious life which I have tried to evoke in this book. Normally, I would end my acknowledgements here. But a word of thanks must be said to our children, Mia and Enan. During the time I spent preparing the lectures upon which this book is based, they were even more encouraging and helpful than usual. Both of them performed all sorts of tasks on my behalf – assisting me with university administrative work, providing secretarial assistance, and zealously protecting me from interruptions. Mia sought out and photocopied several rare items for me from Brandeis University Library's superb Judaica collection. I give thanks to Him Who "turns the heart of the fathers to the children, and turns the heart of the children to their fathers."

July 1995 N.A.S.

INTRODUCTION

Over the past two hundred years, the Jewish people — like the world around it — has undergone a radical transformation, or more precisely, a number of radical transformations. For the greater part of the eighteenth century, most Jews — Ashkenazim and Sephardim alike — lived in semi-autonomous, corporate communities amidst the larger societies around them. In some places, they were viewed as aliens or pariahs, confined to ghettoes or a pale of settlement, or at the least restricted from living in certain locales without special permission. In other places, they were protégés, "protected subjects" (*servi in camera* in Christendom, *ahl al-dhimma* in the Domain of Islam), often, but not necessarily, living in their own quarters or neighborhoods either by force of law or by custom. But everywhere they were politically, socially, religiously and, ultimately, culturally, *the other*.

During the late eighteenth and early nineteenth centuries, the new ideas of the Enlightenment, together with new modes of thought, began to penetrate small circles of Western and Central European Jews, most of whom were Ashkenazim. (The process had begun somewhat earlier among the smaller Sephardi communities of the West.) During this same period, the walls of the ghetto began to come down and the Jews began to enter the social, economic, and political life of the wider society. The largest traditional centers of Jewish population, also Ashkenazi, in Eastern Europe started to undergo this metamorphosis in the late eighteenth century, but the process was more uneven and spasmodic than in Western Europe.

The other great branch of world Jewry, the Sephardi and Oriental Jews, living mainly in the Islamic lands of North Africa, the Balkans, and the Near East, regions that lagged behind the West in their economic and technological development, also began to be touched by the winds of change only about a generation or so after their Eastern European brethren.

The transformation of the Sephardi and Oriental Jews was far more gradual and chequered than was the case even in Eastern Europe, and in some places had barely begun even by the nineteen forties. The reason for this is that the phenomena which are subsumed under the notion of modernity arose in Europe and only spread into the Islamic world as that region was drawn into increasing contact with the West and gradually but inexorably came under its hegemony.

Jews responded to the challenges, opportunities, and problems that the modern era presented to them in a variety of ways that ran the gamut from a rejection of all that was new and a turning inward to a more intensified exclusivism, at one end of the spectrum, to a total rejection of everything in the Jewish tradition and indeed of Jewish identity itself via assimilation, at the other end. In between these two poles, there were many gradations of response that included modern religious movements of all stripes (neo-traditionalist, quasi-traditionalist, and anti-traditionalist) and secularist movements (Yiddish culturalism, Jewish socialism, and, most important of all, Zionism).

Most studies of Jewish modernity have dealt with the responses of Western Jewry — primarily Ashkenazi Jewry — to the modern condition. Indeed, most books of any sort on the Jews in the modern world deal in the main with Ashkenazim. This book is intended, like all of my studies, to correct in some measure this imbalance. It is about some of the varied responses of Sephardi and Oriental Jewry to modernity, specifically some of their religious responses. The points of comparison and contrast to the larger and more intensively examined Ashkenazi world are, I believe, not merely interesting, but highly instructive. For what they show are two different models of modern religious development resulting from two different historical experiences. In general, Sephardi and Oriental Jewry made the transition into modern times while preserving its equilibrium far more more successfully than had European Jewish society upon its emergence from the ghetto, and they were better able to preserve some of their existential moorings. The entire modernizing process was overall more gradual and less traumatic for Eastern Jews than it was for their Ashkenazi brethren or indeed for their Muslim neighbors. Although the Westernizing forces of modernity came to the Sephardi and Oriental Jews primarily from without, the religious evolution of these communities developed from within. Their coming to terms with the modern world did not continually lead to a stark and invidious choice between traditional religion and progress as was the case for so much of Ashkenazi Jewry

Eastern Jewry produced no Reform Judaism,[1] no Historical-Positivism, no neo-Orthodoxy, no ultra-Orthodoxy. Neither, for that matter, did it produce an anti-religious Jewish movement. Right up until the mass exodus of these Jews in the mid-twentieth century, the Sephardi religious responses to the challenges of a world of unprecedented change came primarily from within the tradition itself, thus preserving both the viability and the integrity of Sephardi Judaism. Anomie, which was one of the characteristic ills of Western modernity, does not seem to have afflicted significant numbers of Sephardi and Oriental Jews while they remained in their ancestral lands.

Judaism — like Islam, but in contradistinction to Christianity — is a religious civilization governed by a sacred law that is held in part to be divinely revealed and in part divinely inspired. Rabbis are first and foremost interpreters of that law. Hence, many of the religious responses surveyed in Chapters One and Two of this book are of a legal rather than a purely theological nature (although theology in Judaism may be implicit or explicit in rendering a judgment of law). Questions that arose with respect to the content of a Jew's education, the permissibility of

[1] That is not to say that there were not religiously reform-minded individuals in the Eastern Jewish world. Indeed, two such individuals are principal subjects of Chapter Two of this book. Nevertheless, the title of a recent and very interesting article about the activities of a reforming rabbi in nineteenth century Syria is somewhat misleading. See Yaron Harel, "A Spiritual Agitation in the East — The Founding of a Reform Community in Aleppo in 1862," *Hebrew Union College Annual* 63 (1992), pp. 15–35 [in Hebrew].

making use of certain conveniences of modern technology on sabbaths and holidays or for ritual purposes, the implications of modern scientific knowledge on customary practice, how to deal with new social realities, including changing public mores — all of these in Judaism are legal questions that require legal answers.

The Sephardi rabbinate had a long record of strong communal leadership and juridical authority that was officially recognized under the Muslim social and political system. The Sephardi rabbis had demonstrated throughout history, on the whole, greater boldness and innovativeness in their legal decision-making than their rabbinical counterparts in Europe. And they continued in these accustomed roles well into the modern period even when their authority came to be based more upon traditional deference and moral suasion than upon full legal autonomy granted by the Gentile authorities.[2]

Although law has a central place in traditional Jewish religiosity, the Sephardi rabbis discussed in this book were not merely jurists. They were also communal leaders who ministered to the spiritual and moral needs of their people. Unlike their Ashkenazi counterparts, they had for their flock not just a smaller or larger sub-group within the broader Jewish community, but the Jewish community as a whole. Some of them at least grasped the unique dilemmas posed for the Jewish layman by modern times and tried to offer some form of guidance. The lives and work of two such perceptive individuals are treated in Chapter Two.

In addition to a preoccupation with law, the yearning for redemption and a love for the land of Israel have occupied a central position in Jewish religiosity, and Sephardi and Oriental

---

[2] See, for example the important observations of the historian of Jewish law, Menachem Elon, regarding the legal creativity of Sephardi scholars in North Africa from the eighteenth century to the present (and these observations have validity for other parts of the Sephardi diaspora as well.) Menachem Elon, "Yiḥudah shel Halakha ve-Ḥevra be-Yahadut Ṣefon Afriqa mi-le'aḥar Gerush Sefarad ve-ʿad Yamenu," in *Halakha u-Fetiḥut Hakhme Moroqo ke-Foseqim le-Dorenu,* ed. Moshe Bar-Yuda (ha-Merkaz le-Tarbut ule-Ḥinnukh shel ha-Histadrut: Tel-Aviv, 1985), pp. 15–38.

Jews shared the same messianic hope as did Jews everywhere throughout the history of the Diaspora. During the nineteenth century, some European Jews under the impact of the new post-Enlightenment antisemitism and under the influence of contemporary nationalism redirected their traditional messianic impulses into a movement for Jewish political and cultural revival — Zionism. (Other Western Jews who sought complete integration into the nations in which they resided responded in a quite contrary fashion, renouncing the political aspects of traditional messianism in favor of a completely spiritualized universalism.) Founded in Europe, the Zionist enterprise in both its secular and religious forms remained essentially Ashkenazi in character right up to the establishment of the State of Israel in 1948, and the culture of the new state reflected specifically European (that is, Ashkenazi) Jewish responses to modernity.

Yet there were also fresh manifestations of a cultural and national revival within some quarters of the Sephardi and Oriental Jewish world during the nineteenth century. Initially these stirrings may have been due to totally traditional factors such as messianic speculation, but already by the end of the first half of the nineteenth century, they had the character of responses to identifiably modern stimuli. Given the very different nature of Eastern Jewish society and its more gradual modernizing experience within a general society that remained highly traditional, these stirrings were generally of a different character than those that evolved into European Zionism. Unlike the latter, Sephardi Zionism began and developed in a primarily religious milieu, or at least in a milieu that accorded religion and traditional norms a considerable measure of respect. Even in its secular manifestations, Sephardi Zionism was — unlike European Zionism — never (and no less importantly never perceived itself to be) in revolt against traditional Judaism. Hence the almost complete absence of religious opposition to Zionism among the Sephardi rabbinate.

Not only did the notion of Jewish national revival have the approval of much of the religious elite in the Sephardi world, but it also enjoyed the deep sympathy of the masses. Yet despite the strength of these sentiments, they did not translate into any sort of widespread, effective, grassroots movement in most places. Nor was there much activity on behalf of the official World Zionist Organization, even though it and its leadership were held in great reverence by many Sephardi and Oriental Jews. Sephardi Zionism, at first for cultural and later for political reasons, remained in most cases passive in nature until the Second World War. This apparent passivity ought not to mask the substantiality of Zionism in the consciousness of Sephardi and Oriental Jews. It must be remembered that they had had little previous experience with political and social activism. Moreover, many of them lived in countries where rising Islamic hostility or the suspicion of colonial authorities made overt Zionist activity during the period between the two world wars imprudent at the very least and perilous at the very worst. The character and the evolution of their Zionism as a genuine and indigenous religious response to modernity is discussed in Chapter Three.

The mass migration of the overwhelming majority of Sephardi and Oriental Jews in the mid-twentieth century to the newborn State of Israel and secondarily to France (and in much less significant numbers to other countries in Europe and the Americas) marked the most abrupt, radical, and undoubtedly traumatic transformation that these Jews had undergone in their one-hundred-and-fifty year encounter with modernity. Rebuilding their lives in completely new surroundings, they were forced to meet a variety of challenges. This was especially true in Israel, where the Sephardim became part of a unique social and political experiment, the reestablishment of a Jewish state after nearly two millennia of dispersion. (Those who went to France came primarily from former French colonial territories in North Africa and had undergone some greater or lesser degree of Gallic acculturation.)

The Sephardim who went to Israel found themselves in a national polity that defined itself as Jewish and in which the Jewish religion was given a state-sanctioned establishment status despite the manifest secularism, indeed irreligiosity, of most of the founding fathers and of the Zionist modern Hebrew culture they had created. There were some religious Jews among the ruling elite, but they, like the secular founders, were mainly European Ashkenazim. The general culture of the Ashkenazi Jews, both secular and religious, was markedly different from that of the Sephardi newcomers. Although they welcomed the latter, they regarded them as exotic and culturally backward. The religious Ashkenazim and Sephardim had, of course, shared elements of the traditional religion in common, but their respective styles of religiosity differed in many ways. Since the Ashkenazi Israelis saw themselves as absorbing the Sephardi and Oriental newcomers, they encouraged them to assimilate into Israeli Jewish society. The secular majority held out an entirely new model of Jewish culture devoid of religion in the traditional sense. (There is a form of civil religion in Israel in which the sabbath is an official day of rest and the Jewish holidays are national holidays.) The religious elite encouraged the newcomers to remain traditionally observant but to abandon those customs and practices that were specific to their diaspora communities and not part of universally shared Jewish heritage. Chapter Four examines how the Sephardi and Oriental Jews, after their initial culture shock, responded to what for many was not their encounter with modernity (as is commonly supposed), but — to use Lyotard's phrase (albeit not exactly in the same sense that he used it) — their "post-modern condition."[3]

The Sephardi and Oriental Jews in Israel (and to a certain extent their brethren in France as well) have responded to their new condition in a wide variety of ways. On the one hand, there has been a widespread decline in strict religious observance

[3] Jean-François Lyotard, *The Post Modern Condition: A Report on Knowledge*, trans. Geoff Bennington and Brian Massumi (University of Minnesota Press: Minneapolis, 1989). See also the discussion of this notion in Anthony Giddens, *The Consequences of Modernity* (Stanford University Press: Stanford, 1990), pp. 45–53.

without a concomitant alienation from religion. Many Sephardim, while not punctillious in fulfilling the 613 commandments, maintain many religious traditions. There is also a vigorous reassertion of certain aspects of popular religion, particularly the veneration of holy men and pilgrimage to their grave sites. This has in recent years taken on proportions exceeding anything that had existed prior to the mass exodus of Sephardi and Oriental Jewry at mid-century. And finally, there is the adoption by some Sephardim of Ashkenazified styles of religiosity ranging from the tutelage of the Lithuanian yeshiva world of a new Sephardi rabbinical elite at one end of the spectrum, through the missionary activities of the Lubavitcher Ḥasidim among the Sephardi masses at the other end. The reassertion of some popular religious practices may be viewed as an attempt at what David Gross has called "reappropriating tradition through its traces." Whereas both the revived popular practices and the adoption of Ashkenazi-style fundamentalism may be seen as a part of a much wider late-twentieth century "demodernizing" revolt found among many societies and religions that is born out of disappointment and disillusionment with modernity in the postmodern age.[4]

[4] David Gross, *The Past in Ruins: Tradition and the Critique of Modernity* (University of Massachusetts Press: Amherst, 1992), pp. 92–106. Concerning "demodernizing consciousness," see Peter L. Berger, Brigitte Berger, and Hansfried Kellner, *The Homeless Mind: Modernization and Consciousness* (Random House: New York, 1973), pp. 201–230.

ONE

The Wind in the Palace: The Initial Responses of Sephardim and Ashkenazim Compared

In 1810, the great Hasidic master, Rabbi Naḥman of Bratslav, reflected upon the revolutionary changes sweeping over Europe and threatening the very existence of his traditional world with the following parable:

> There was once a time says the master of prayer when each of us had gone to his own special place. The warrior, the orator, and all of the king's men — each had gone to renew his particular strength.
>
> At that time a great windstorm swept over the world. The entire earth was confounded; dry land was transformed into sea and sea into dry land, deserts came up where there had been towns, and new towns sprang up in areas where there had been only desert. The whole world was turned upside down by that wind.
>
> When the wind came into the king's palace, it did no damage at all. As it whipped through the palace, however, it grabbed up the beautiful child and carried him away, all in an instant. The king's daughter ran off in pursuit of her child. Soon she was followed by her mother, the queen, and then by the king himself. Thus all of them were scattered, and nobody knows their place.
>
> None of us was there when this happened, as we each had gone off to renew our strength. When we did return to the palace, we found no one there.... Since then we have all been scattered, and none of us can now get back to that place where he needs to go to renew his strength. Since the wind came and turned the entire world around, changing land into sea and sea into land, the old paths are no longer of any use. We are now in need of new paths, because all the places have been altered. Meanwhile, we cannot renew our former strength. We do however retain an imprint of those former times and that in itself is very great.[1]

The windstorm in Rabbi Naḥman's tale was not only the Napoleonic armies sweeping across Europe at that time and

[1] Arthur Green, *Tormented Master: A Life of Rabbi Nahman of Bratslav* (The University of Alabama Press: Alabama, 1979), pp. 248–249.

overturning the old political order, but the winds of radical social and intellectual change represented by the Enlightenment and the French Revolution. Rabbi Naḥman, envisaged an ensuing spiritual chaos in which the well-known paths to God were devastated or abandoned and Jews would be unable to find their way.

The world transformed by the powerful forces symbolized by Rabbi Naḥman's whirlwind is the modern world. The transformations had begun in Western European society in the preceding century. However, they had only begun to penetrate German Jewry during the last third of the eighteenth century with, among other things, the advent of Moses Mendelssohn and the Haskala, and they were only now coming into direct contact with the vast majority of Ashkenazi Jews living in Eastern Europe.[2]

Throughout the nineteenth century, the entire structure of the premodern European Jewish world crumbled. Traditional communal authority vanished de jure with Emancipation and de facto with mass defections from halakhic Judaism to secularism or out of the Jewish fold altogether. For many religious leaders, such as Rabbi Naḥman, the transition to modernity was nothing short of a catastrophe. As Jacob Katz has observed, it would be "some time before they could rally their forces sufficiently to present a systematic answer that took into account all the ingredients of the new reality and, despite them, maintained the validity of tradition."[3]

---

[2] The best introductions to European Jewish society on the eve of modern times and its encounter with modernity are Jacob Katz, *Tradition and Crisis: Jewish Society at the End of the Middle Ages*, 2nd ed., trans. Bernard Dov Cooperman (New York University Press: New York, 1993); and idem, *Out of the Ghetto: The Social Background of Jewish Emancipation, 1770–1870* (Harvard University Press: Cambridge, Mass., 1973). For a view that pushes the transformational forces among Ashkenazi Jewry back by several generations, see Azriel Shochat, *Beginnings of the Haskalah among German Jewry* (Bialik Institute: Jerusalem, 1960) [Hebrew].

[3] Jacob Katz, *Out of the Ghetto*, p. 142.

The earliest religious response to modernity was anti-traditionalist in the body of the Reform movement. It denied the eternal validity of the halakha which had hitherto governed all aspects of Jewish life and instituted major changes in liturgical practice.[4] The challenge of Reform and of the more general Jewish Enlightenment (Haskala) did eventually stimulate a response from the champions of the traditional faith. The earliest traditionalist response was one of uncompromising reaction, summed up in the rallying cry of Rabbi Moses Sofer of Pressburg, known as the Ḥatam Sofer — "*he-ḥadash asur min ha-Torah be-khol maqom*" ("Whatever is new is forbidden by the Torah in every instance").[5] This reactionary stance remained the essential position for a large segment of traditionalists, and it was only in the course of the nineteenth century, primarily in Germany, that there developed a modernist neo-Orthodoxy which could embrace the positive aspects of modern secular culture while affirming loyalty to traditional religious practice and theology.[6]

As a result of the process of modernization, Ashkenazi Jewry — which is now concentrated in North America, Western Europe, and Israel — is split today into irreconcilable religious camps, on the one hand, and a large body (in many places the majority) of secularized Jews of greater or less ethnicity, on the other.

The other great branch of world Jewry — the Sephardim, or to be more precise, Sephardi and Oriental Jewry — offers an instructive point of contrast to the Ashkenazi experience in their

---

[4] For a historical survey of the Reform movement, see Michael A. Meyer, *Response to Modernity: A History of the Reform Movement in Judaism* (Oxford University Press: New York and Oxford, 1988).

[5] The dictum comes from the Mishna ʿOrla 3:9 and refers to new agricultural produce. Concerning Sofer, see Jacob Katz, "Towards a Biography of the Hatam Sofer," in *From East and West: Jews in a Changing Europe, 1750–1870,* ed. Frances Malino and David Sorkin (Basil Blackwell: Oxford and Cambridge, Mass., 1990, pp. 223–266.

[6] For the rise and evolution of this trend, see Mordechai Breuer, *Modernity within Tradition: The Social History of Orthodox Jewry in Imperial Germany,* trans. Elizabeth Petuchowski (Columbia University Press: New York, 1992).

encounter with modern times. The Western Sephardim in the Netherlands, Hamburg, Germany, France, England, and the New World — many of whom were *conversos* who returned to Judaism after imbibing Renaissance culture — were sociologically the first modern Jews. That is, they were the first Jews to dress in the fashion of their Gentile neighbors, to adopt their language and many aspects of their lifestyle, and to take part in the intellectual and political life of the non-Jewish communities around them. It was from this Western Sephardi milieu that there sprang Benedict Spinoza, the seventeenth-century rationalist and freethinker, who was one of the first to lay the groundwork for Higher Criticism of the Bible.[7] The great majority of Sephardi Jews settled in the lands of Islam after their Expulsion from Iberia. In many places they rose to dominance over the indigenous Jewish communities. In many other places they eventually fused with the local Jewries. In some localities, they maintained a separate existence. But everywhere, their impact was great, and one can with justification refer to the Jews of the Middle East and North Africa (who are commonly called in contemporary Hebrew *ha-Sefaradim ve-ʿEdot ha-Mizraḥ*, or "the Iberians and the Communities of the East") as an organic — although by no means monolithic — entity sharing similar liturgical, legal and customary traditions. Unlike the Western Sephardim, they lived outside the early centers of modernity. Indeed, the modernizing forces that affected their Central and Eastern European Ashkenazi brethren came to them later still, beginning a generation or so after. As we shall see, the winds of change that swept over them, did so under dissimilar historical circumstances, over a longer period time, and with different results. In my book *The Jews of Arab Lands in Modern Times*,[8] I surveyed

[7] It is interesting to note that another of the forerunners of modern biblical criticism, the French Huguenot, Jean Astruc (1684–1766), was probably also of Sephardi origin See M. H. Shulewitz, "Astruc, Jean," *Encyclopaedia Judaica* 3, col. 809.

[8] Jewish Publication Society: Philadelphia, 1991.

the social and political evolution of Middle Eastern and North African Jewry during the nineteenth and twentieth centuries. What I would like to do here is examine some of the specifically religious responses of these Jews to the challenges of modernity as they encountered it.

Oriental Jewry's confrontation with modernity was a direct result of the impact of an ascendant Europe upon the economic, political, and cultural life of the Islamic world from the end of the eighteenth century onwards. Here lies the first essential difference in the very nature of the modernizing process as experienced by European Ashkenazi Jewry and Middle Eastern Sephardi Jewry. In the case of the former, the modernizing process resulted from the breaking down of age-old barriers that had separated them from the surrounding majority society. For the latter, the process was the result of the intrusion of external forces into their world. For European Jewry, modern times marked the almost complete breakdown of traditional communal organization and authority. For Middle Eastern and North African Jewry, this was not entirely the case. Confessional groups (the so-called millets) remained officially recognized corporate entities within society throughout the period of the Tanzimat (literally, "reorganization") reforms in the nineteenth- and early twentieth-century Ottoman Empire. This remained the case even after the First World War in most Muslim countries, whether they were under outright colonial rule, foreign protectorates, or newly independent states.[9]

One of the most striking differences between European and Middle Eastern Jewries' encounter with modernity was in the overall response of their respective religious leaderships. As a rule, the rabbis of the Middle East and North Africa, most of whom belonged to the Sephardi elite, demonstrated a far more non-confrontational attitude to the social, economic, and techno-

---

[9] See Stillman, *The Jews of Arab Lands in Modern Times*, pp. 9–10, 56–62, and 301.

logical changes taking place around them than did their counterparts in Europe. This is not to say that the rabbis in the Islamic world were happy with some of the concomitant tendencies towards the phenomenon of modernity, such as a decline in the strictness of religious observance and in Jewish learning, as well as laxer moral and social behavior among the laity. The Sephardi and Oriental rabbinical literature of the late nineteenth and early twentieth century is full of complaints about the erosion of decorum in the synagogue, the lowering of inhibitions in public conduct, and the weakening of discipline in the patriarchal family. "Woe to the eyes that see such things and to the ears that hear them," exclaims the Aleppan Chief Rabbi Jacob Saul Dwek shortly before the First World War, referring to Jewish families attending cabarets and Jewish girls singing and dancing in them. "Our eyes are darkened at seeing the evil which has befallen our people," laments Rabbi Elijah Bekhor Ḥazzan, the Ḥakham Bashi of Alexandria, at what he considers the immodest evening dresses worn by well-to-do Jewish women and the practice of mixed dancing which were becoming commonplace around the turn of the century. "We are heartsick," bemoans the Baghdadi preacher Rabbi Simeon Agasi, in a sermon delivered in 1913 against the public flouting of the sabbath, the dietary laws, and traditional standards of morality by some of the more westernized members of the community.[10]

Although the rabbis of the Middle East and North Africa were deeply disturbed by what they considered to be some of the negative consequences of Western cultural influences, they were not against modern civilization per se. They understood that there was much that was positive that could be learned from

[10] Jacob Saul Dwek, *Derekh Emuna* (Aleppo, 1913/14), p. 17b; Elijah Ḥazzan, *Taʿalumot Lev*, vol. 3 (Farag Ḥayyim Mizraḥi: Alexandria, 1902/3), 58b; Simeon Agasi, *Imre Shimʿon* (Jerusalem, 1967/68), pp. 124–144. For further examples of rabbinic unhappiness with the decline in religious observance and traditional values, see Stillman, *The Jews of Arab Lands in Modern Times*, pp. 36–37, and the sources cited there in notes 33–35.

Europe. "If in each generation we were to forbid everything that has newly appeared among the uncircumcised and the Gentiles, then we would be forbidding even some permissible things," writes Elijah Ḥazzan in one of his responsa.[11]

Indeed almost from the very beginning, despite certain reservations, the Oriental rabbis generally took a permissive stance with regard to the new western-style education that was becoming available during the course of the nineteenth century. At first, this new education consisted primarily of the study of European languages which many native Jews and Christians considered necessary in order to take advantage of expanding opportunities as their region was being drawn ineluctably into the world economic system. Quite naturally, the rabbis were opposed to Christian missionaries teaching Jewish children — or adults for that matter. In 1846, the rabbis of Baghdad went so far as to pronounce a *ḥerem*, (a ban of excommunication) upon anyone who studied with English missionaries, but this was clearly an exceptional response which came only after two of the students began attending Christian services at the mission.[12] More typical of the early rabbinical reaction to foreign language education was that of Rabbi Israel Moses Ḥazzan, a leading Sephardi scholar of the nineteenth century, who was the Ḥakham Bashi (Chief Rabbi) of Alexandria from 1857 until his death in 1863. In his fascinating book *She'erit ha-Naḥala* (The Remnant of the Inheritance), which is cast in the form of dialogue between a learned and pious merchant (*ha-soḥer*) and a pair of rabbinic scholars (*ha-ḥakhamim*), Rabbi Ḥazzan discusses, *inter alia*, the question of language study by Jewish youths. While arguing that Hebrew and Arabic are the most important

---

[11] Hazzan, *Ta'alumot Lev*, vol. 3, p. 59a.

[12] The missionaries, themselves converted Jews, appealed to the British consul for assistance, citing their rights as Englishmen. See Public Records Office (London) FO 195/237, excerpts from which are published in Stillman, *The Jews of Arab Lands*, pp. 377–383.

languages for Jewish children in the Middle East, the rabbi, speaking through the scholars, maintains that "Indeed it was never forbidden at any place or at any time for the sons of Judah to learn the languages of the nations."[13] However, he states that it is preferable that the teachers be Jews themselves. If they are Gentiles, they should be employees of the Jewish community, and they should not be clergymen or missionaries. Speaking through his fictional scholars, Rabbi Ḥazzan also argued that Jews should study secular subjects including the physical sciences which contain much that is valuable and worthwhile knowing.[14]

Moses Ḥazzan's contemporary, Rabbi Isaac Bengualíd in Tetouan, Morocco, also believed in the permissibility of secular studies, particularly language education. In a responsum to a query from the Jewish community of neighboring Gibraltar, most of whose members were of northern Moroccan origin, Rabbi Bengualíd ruled that it was permissible for the Jewish school to accept government subsidies for language instruction. The money, however, could not be used for religious subjects since it was improper to use money from Gentile sources for sacred purposes.[15]

The open attitude of the Sephardi rabbis toward the introduction of secular subjects into the Jewish school curriculum stands in marked contrast to the attitude of the Ashkenazi religious leadership in Eastern Europe at this time, especially in Czarist Russia, where attempts by the authorities to introduce secular studies into traditional ḥeders and yeshivas, as well as to

---

[13] Israel Moses Ḥazzan, *She'erit ha-Naḥala: Viku'aḥ. Sho'el u-Meshiv* (Tipografia Ottolenghi: Alexandria, 1862), p. 11, para. 40. Concerning this interesting figure and his thought, see José Faur, *Ha-Rav Yisra'el Moshe Ḥazzan: ha-Ish u-Mishnato* (Raphael Arbel Academic Publishers: Haifa, 1978).

[14] Ibid., p. 12, para. 40 (Gentile teachers); p. 24, para. 85 (secular subjects).

[15] Isaac Bengualíd, *Va-Yomer Yiṣḥaq* (Jerusalem, 1977/78), no. 99. See also Marc D. Angel, *Voices in Exile: A Study in Sephardi Intellectual History* (Ktav Publishing House: Hoboken, New Jersey, 1991), pp. 182–183.

establish state-run modern schools, were viewed — correctly in the Russian case — as government ploys for undermining Judaism. The great Volozhin yeshiva, for example, closed in 1892 rather than introduce general subjects.[16]

The principal disseminator of modern, western-style education among the Jews of the Islamic world was the Alliance Israélite Universelle, the first international Jewish welfare organization founded in Paris in 1860, which by the end of the nineteenth century had established schools in every major town and city with a Jewish community from Morocco to Iran. As an organization under the auspices of benevolent coreligionists, the Alliance aroused little suspicion. Although the Alliance's instructional program was primarily secularist, it did include a not insignificant Judaic component which in the early days was taught by local rabbis and teachers. Most religious leaders initially gave the Alliance their support, and despite occasional instances of friction, usually caused by the over-zealous or impolitic behavior of a particular schoolmaster, many leading rabbis sent their children to Alliance schools. Rabbi Elijah Bekhor Ḥazzan, the Ḥakham Bashi of Alexandria and a leading halakhic authority, sent his own son to the Alliance school and took him out only with great regret in 1904 because the boy had been beaten on several occasions by the schoolmaster. (He then placed his son in a non-Jewish European school — presumably a secular one — rather than send him to a Jewish institution in another city.) The Iraqi sage, Rabbi ʿAbd Allah Somekh, allowed

---

[16] For Eastern European Jewish resistance to state sponsored attempts at introducing secular education, see Simon M. Dubnov, *History of the Jews in Russian and Poland from the Earliest Times until the Present Day*, transl. I. Friedlaender (Jewish Publication Society: Philadelphia, 1916–1920), vol. II, pp. 52–59 and 175; also Menachem Friedman, "Ḥaredim Confront the Modern City," *Studies in Contemporary Jewry* II, ed. Peter Y. Medding (Indiana University Press: Bloomington, 1986), p. 95, n. 11.

his grandson to attend the Alliance school in Baghdad In fact, according to family recollections, he insisted upon it.[17]

The only example of all-out, implacable religious opposition to the Alliance, and indeed to all modern schooling, came from the rabbis of the zealous island community of Jerba, Tunisia. But all observers of Jerban Jewry over the past century and a half have noted the exceptional nature of its religiosity which bears certain resemblences of style to that of Lithuanian Misnagdic Jewry. In addition to its geographical insularity being a possible factor in Jerban Jewry's isolationism, there may also be some influence from the surrounding Ibadi Kharijite milieu which cultivates a strict ideal of communal separation from mainstream Sunni Islam.[18]

It is interesting to note that throughout the nineteenth century there were very few indigenous attempts to establish modern Jewish religious schools in Muslim countries. The most notable exception was Ḥakham Zaki Cohen's boarding school in Beirut, Tiferet Yisra'el, which operated from the 1870s until 1904. In addition to a traditional Judaic curriculum, the school taught modern languages, including Arabic, Turkish, French, and German. The school attracted students from as far away as

---

[17] See Stillman, *The Jews of Arab Lands in Modern Times*, pp. 35 and 241–242. For cases of schoolmasters alienating local rabbis, see ibid., pp. 34–35, and sources cited there in n. 26. Harvey Goldberg incorrectly assesses the scope of local rabbinical opposition to the Alliance schools in his article "Religious Responses Among North African Jews in the Nineteenth and Twentieth Centuries," in *The Uses of Tradition: Jewish Continuity in the Modern Era*, ed. Jack Wertheimer (Jewish Theological Seminary of America: New York and Jerusalem, 1992), p. 124. I am grateful to Sylvia G. Haim, a great granddaughter of Rabbi Somekh, for the information about her ancestor (oral communication, London, March 1, 1994).

[18] See Abraham L. Udovitch and Lucette Valensi, *The Last Arab Jews: The Communities of Jerba, Tunisia* (Harwood Academic Publishers: New York, 1984), pp. 87–88; and for some humorous contemporary observations, Nahum Slouschz, *Travels in North Africa* (Jewish Publication Society: Philadelphia, 1927), pp. 253–255.

Istanbul and Izmir.[19] Even during the first half of the twentieth century, efforts to develop modern religiously oriented schools were rare. Mori Yiḥye Qafiḥ's Dar Daᶜ (Hebrew *dor deᶜa* — "generation of knowledge") school in Sanᶜa, which combined a Torah education with secular subjects and the study of Turkish and Arabic, was open only between 1909 and 1913. More successful was the Em ha-Banim network of schools in Morocco founded in 1917. These schools which operated throughout the entire Protectorate period in Fez, Sefrou, and Marrakesh, although run and supported by Moroccans, were, however, founded at the urging of a European rabbi, Wolf Hilperine, who had come to Morocco from London.[20]

The probable reason that there were so few indigenous attempts to establish modern religious schools — indeed any modern Jewish schools — is that most Jews in the Muslim world, including the religious leaders, perceived modern education, like modernity itself, as something to be acquired from its genuine Western source.

The Sephardi religious leadership's response to modernity was not merely one of passive acceptance, as in the case of the new western-style schools that proliferated throughout the Oriental Jewish world during the second half of the nineteenth and the first half of the twentieth centuries. Rather it was also one of active and creative engagement.

The rabbis of the East had a long tradition of communal leadership and juridical authority that was legally recognized under the Islamic social and political system. Historically, the majority of the great *poseqim* (decisors of Jewish law), from the Babylonian geonim to Isaac al-Fasi, Maimonides, and Joseph

---

[19] Hayyim J. Cohen, *The Jews of the Middle East, 1860–1972* (John Wiley & Sons: New York and Toronto, 1973), pp. 135–136.

[20] David Ovadia, *La Communauté de Sefrou,* vol. 3 (Makhon le-Ḥeqer Toldot Qehillot Yehude Maroqo: Jerusalem, 1975), pp. 212–220 [in Hebrew]; Louis Brunot and Elie Malka, *Textes judéo-arabes de Fès* (Typo-Litho Ecole du Livre: Rabat, 1939), pp. 237–238 and 241, n. 6.

Karo, had come from the Sephardi and Oriental milieu. Unlike their Ashkenazi counterparts who had lived in a much more hostile environment in Christian Europe, they had always been more willing to look beyond the proverbial "four cubits of the law" in their decision making. Also in contradistinction to the Ashkenazi rabbis, they did not face the kind of all-out rebellion against traditional Judaism that became so widespread in Europe as a result of emancipation. The reason for this — as I have already noted — was that the Islamic society in which Oriental Jewry lived was still highly traditional and continued to be divided along ethnoreligious lines. Jews might become westernized in dress, in education, and even in some of their tastes and habits, but with the exception of Algerian Jewry which was under the tutelage of the Parisian General Consistory and which had been granted French citizenship en masse by the Crémieux Decree in 1870, and some highly acculturated individuals elsewhere, few could pretend that they were truly French, British, or Italian, as the case might be. And no one thought of himself as an Arab or a Turk. Most Jews were first and foremost Jews both in their own eyes and in the eyes of others. In contrast to Europe, apostasy from Judaism either to Christianity or Islam was absolutely negligible.[21]

Because it was not faced with an all-out rebellion from within or a delegitimation of its authority from without, the Sephardi rabbinate viewed as one of its principal tasks the preservation of the Jewish communal unity and the spiritual guidance of its members in the new era. Rather than trying to cut off or to restrain those who strayed from the paths of observance, they tried to bring them into some degree of harmony with tradition. There were one or two exceptions to this tolerant approach. In 1906, the rabbis of Aleppo published a ban of anathema upon

[21] There were, of course, one or two exceptions, but the phenomenon was statistically insignificant. See Stillman, *The Jews of Arab Lands in Modern Times*, pp. 20–21 and 245–249.

public Sabbath desecrators, and the rabbis of Tripoli, Libya, published a similar edict in 1911.[22]

More typical of the Oriental rabbinical approach to the task of leadership is that expressed by Rabbi Raphael Aaron Ben Simeon, the Chief Rabbi of Cairo throughout the last decade of the nineteenth century and the first two decades of the twentieth, in a responsum:

> It is incumbent upon the man concerned with his religion and faith, who loves the people of his nation with a pure heart, to exert himself for their welfare and to seek to preserve their purity in whatever way he can find without pulling the cord of strictness to its limit.[23]

An example of the Eastern rabbis' generally tolerant and nuanced approach to increasing secularizing tendencies among members of their community during the second half of the nineteenth century, may be seen in the reaction of the revered Baghdadi spiritual leader, Rabbi Joseph Ḥayyim b. Elijah al Ḥakam (known in both Ashkenazi and Sephardi religious circles today as the Ben Ish Ḥayy) to the practice of Jews frequenting Gentile coffeehouses on the Sabbath. He notes that it is preferable not to spend one's time in such idle pursuits on the holy day and that whoever avoids doing so will attain blessing. As for those who do go, he merely cautions them "to consume only what was prepared prior to their coming." But he adds that he does "not protest vociferously for a number of reasons."[24]

---

[22] Dwek, *Derekh Emuna*, pp. 120a–121a, translated in Stillman, *The Jews of Arab Lands in Modern Times*, pp. 223–224; Central Archive for the History of the Jewish People (Jerusalem) LIB/TR 2990.

[23] Raphael Aaron Ben Simeon, *Umi-Ṣur Devash* (Defus shel ha-R. Samuel ha-Levi Zuckerman: Jerusalem, 1914/1915), p. 111a.

[24] Joseph Ḥayyim, *Ben Ish Ḥayy*, Part 2 (Jerusalem, 1977), p. 48. Concerning this important figure and his *oeuvre*, see Louis Jacobs, "The Responsa of Rabbi Joseph Hayim of Baghdad," in *Perspectives on Jews and Judaism*, ed. A. A. Chiel (Rabbinical Assembly: New York, 1978), pp. 189-214. Jacobs notes that the Ben Ish Ḥayy was "on the whole, very strict with regard to Sabbath observance, following the authorities who hold that one who profanes the Sabbath in public is to be excluded from the Jewish community. On the other hand, he permits the riding of a bicycle on the Sabbath, where there is not an *'eruv*." See Jacobs, ibid., p. 194.

The Ḥakham Bashi Raphael Aaron Ben Simeon reveals a similarly gentle approach in his responsum to the problem of *shaʿaṭnez* (the biblically prohibited mixture of linen and wool) which was commonly found in the new European clothes which by the early twentieth century were being worn by most Jewish men in Egypt. Since there were many Jewish tailors and haberdashers in the country, the question of livelihood (*parnasa*) was an important consideration. The chief rabbi therefore ruled that Jewish tailors may make such suits for Gentiles. If a Jewish client wishes to purchase a garment containing *shaʿaṭnez,* the tailor should warn him. If the client does not care, then the tailor should not him put it on him for the fitting himself, but let the buyer or a non-Jewish employee do it. "And that will suffice."[25]

In another case involving halakhic prescriptions regarding dress, Rabbi Joseph Ḥayyim of Baghdad permits a Jewish pharmacist to remove his *ṭallit qaṭan*, the undershirt with ritual "show fringe" (*ṣiṣit*) on its four corners, when going work. The pharmacist had explained to him that his Gentile colleagues made fun of him because of it when they were changing together into their clinical coats. Although the great Baghdadi scholar's decision is based purely upon halakhic grounds, this was not a minor dispensation since the wearing of a fringed garment was not only a pentateuchal commandment, but in Joseph Ḥayyim's view as a Kabbalist, a mystical observance of the highest order. The exigencies of the non-traditional workplace must therefore have weighed heavily in his thinking even though he does not mention this in his highly technical legal response.[26]

---

[25] Raphael Aaron Ben Simeon, *Nehar Miṣrayim* (Farag Ḥayyim Mizraḥi: Alexandria, 1907/08), p. 128a.

[26] This responsum is cited in Shlomo Deshen, who feels that the Ben Ish Ḥayy is "indifferent to the social and religious predicaments involved in the question. His imagination is fired exclusively by its technical aspect... The responsum reveals how unaware this leader of the community was of the sociocultural ramifications of the problem at hand, unaware of changing times." Shlomo Deshen, "Baghdad Jewry in Late Ottoman Times: The Emergence of Social Classes and of Secularization," *AJS Review* 19:1 (1994), pp. 37–38. I am not so sure.

Plate 1 Rabbi Joseph Ḥayyim of Baghdad (1833–1909), popularly known as the Ben Ish Ḥayy. A leading halakhic and authority and moralist, widely regarded by Sephardi Oriental Jews.

The Sephardi rabbis also approach halakhic questions resulting from the revolutionary new technology of the modern age in a sober fashion without any noticeable alarm. In 1877, Ḥakham ʿAbd Allah Somekh, who was regarded as the supreme halakhic authority by the far-flung Iraqi Jewish mercantile colonies extending from India to the Far East, was asked by a Jew in India whether it was permitted to ride the railway on sabbaths and holidays. In his responsum, Rabbi Somekh rules that within the city limits it is permitted to ride a train; however, it is forbidden to travel between cities because that would violate the Sabbath boundary. It is interesting to note that the Baghdadi sage states that he is aware of this new invention, which did not yet exist in Iraq, from European rabbinical literature (including writings of the Ḥatam Sofer whom he specifically mentions). He was also aware of contrary opinions that were based on such arguments as the inappropriate, profane nature of train riding on a sacred day, but chooses to reject them. For him, modern technology raises technical problems. It is not perceived as part of wider threat.[27]

The Ḥakham Bashi of Cairo, Raphael Aaron Ben Simeon, though not alarmed by technological innovation, betrays a clear awareness that it raises unprecedented questions for religious Jews — questions for which the tradition does not provide easy answers.

[27] ʿAbd Allah Abraham Joseph Somekh, *Zivḥe Ṣedeq,* Part 2 (1986/87), Sec. Shu"T Oraḥ ha-Ḥayyim, no. 23, pp. 25–26. *Shu"T Zivḥe Ṣedeq ha-Ḥadashot,* Part 3 (Makhon Or ha-Mizraḥ: Jerusalem, 1981), pp. 122–124. This particular responsum is also discussed in Zvi Zohar, "The Attitude of Rabbi Abdallah Somekh towards Changes in the Nineteenth Century as Reflected in His Halakhic Writings," *Peʿamim* 36 (1988), pp. 91–92. This would constitute another case in which Deshen would contend that the *poseq* does not see the broader social and religious implications of the new technology. See Deshen, "Baghdad Jewry in Late Ottoman Times," pp. 38–39, n. 23, where he refers specifically to Zohar's article.

Plate 2 Ḥakham ʿAbd Allah Somekh of Baghdad (1813–1889). He was the supreme halakhic authority for the Iraqi Jewish mercantile communities that extended from India to China.

New inventions ... have proliferated in our generation which increased and expanded man's wisdom with regard to the production of sophisticated articles of manufacture by means of knowledge and research into the basic foundations of creation.... Each day new inventions appear, of which our ancestors and forefathers never thought. The task of the teacher to respond to those who question him about these discoveries has become heavier.... For it is difficult to find parallels to them in our holy Talmud from which practical results may be obtained for teaching whether to forbid or to permit.[28]

Living in the Egyptian metropolis which was undergoing rapid modernization during the nineteenth century, Rabbi Ben Simeon felt more acutely how daunting was the task at hand, than did Rabbi Somekh in more provincial Baghdad. But he was not overwhelmed by the challenge, neither did he shrink from it. He soberly declares that in seeking halakhic answers to questions raised by scientific technology,

It is only through great exertion with a clear and undisturbed mind, and at leisure that one can undertake this task and compare each instance ... with its possible parallel in the deep sea of our Talmud. With all of this, perhaps the teacher will succeed in finding some discussion in the tradition which is in accordance with the Halakha.[29]

While recognizing the challenges presented by modern technology, many rabbis appreciated the improvements that such innovations as telegraph, gas, and electricity brought to people's lives. Some of them express their admiration for what is one of the most characteristic features of modernity; namely, the trustworthy, impersonal, and rationalized nature of the bureaucracies that operated these services. Thus, for example, the mail service, in the view of Rabbis Elijah Ḥazzan and Raphael Aaron Ben Simeon, is a ritually fit medium for sending a bill of divorce (*geṭ*) from afar. The impersonal bureaucratic nature of the post does not place it within the halakhically forbidden category of a Gentile agent even though the postal workers themselves are primarily non-Jews. Rabbi ʿAbd Allah Somekh in Baghdad and

[28] Raphael Aaron Ben Simeon, *Umi-Ṣur Devash*, p. 23a.
[29] Ibid.

Rabbi Raphael Aaron Ben Simeon in Cairo are both quite eloquent in praising the rationalized bureaucracy of the telegraph agency and rule along with many other *poseqim* of the period that it is a fit medium for transmitting certain types of valid witness from Jews even though the telegram itself has been transmitted by non-Jewish employees and does not bear the actual signature of the sender. The high degree of trust that is placed by the rabbis in this impersonal system is surely to be considered in and of itself an important psychological consequence of modernity.[30]

Some of the Oriental rabbis even envisage the potential of modern technology for solving certain halakhic problems. As one of them writes, "It occurred to me that we might fill this gap with God's help by means of a modern contemporary invention."[31]

This generally positive attitude on the part of Oriental rabbis toward the technology and skills of the West stands in marked contrast to many Muslim religious leaders at that time, who regarded everything connected with the penetration of modern Western civilization as a threat. Even the Islamic religious

---

[30] Elijah Ḥazzan, *Taʿalumot Lev,* vol. 2, p. 61a. ʿAbd Allah Somekh, *Shu"t Zivḥe Ṣedeq ha-Ḥadashot,* pp. 47–51, Sec. 26 (This responsum is also discussed at length in Zohar, "The Attitude of Rabbi Abdallah Somekh towards Changes in the Nineteenth Century as Reflected in His Halakhic Writings," pp. 96–98); Raphael Aaron Ben Simeon, *Umi- Ṣur Devash,* p. 75a. See also Elijah Ḥazzan's eloquent words concerning the telegraph in his *Neve Shalom* (Farag Ḥayyim Mizraḥi: Alexandria, 1994), p. 45a. Concerning the notion of trust in abstract systems, see Anthony Giddens, *The Consequences of Modernity* (Stanford University Press: Standford, California, 1990), pp. 83–88; and also Peter L. Berger, Brigitte Berger, and Hansfried Kellner, *The Homeless Mind: Modernization and Consciousness* (Random House: New York, 1973), pp. 41–62.

[31] Raphael Ben Simeon, *Umi-Ṣur Devash,* p. 39a. Rabbi Ben Simeon is referring to the mechanism of the French-built water works in Cairo which supplied water from the Nile to homes throughout the city. He was hoping that this could solve the problem in a country with no rainfall of establishing ritual baths (*mikvehs*) in the new suburbs where many Jews now lived. He made a careful study of the machinery and even presents a detailed cross section of the apparatus with his responsum.

reformers who appeared in the late nineteenth and early twentieth centuries, such as Jamal al-Din al-Afghani, Muḥammad ʿAbduh, and Rashid Riḍa, saw the utilitarian elements of modernity primarily in terms of strengthening Islam in its struggle against the West.[32] This marked contrast between the stances of the Sephardi rabbis and the Muslim ʿulama' toward the new technology was predicated upon their opposing perceptions of the West generally. For the Jews of the Islamic world (including the rabbis), the West — or more precisely the Western powers and their emancipated Jewries — had for some time represented a benevolent force to which the Jewish communities of North Africa and the Levant had been turning for assistance and protection. They were, therefore, more positively predisposed toward the changes wrought by Western influences. There may also have been — at least in the case of some rabbis — an element of Middle Eastern fatalism, that dictated a degree of acceptance of the realities of the new era, without necessarily acquiescing to those aspects which they deemed unacceptable.

For the Sephardi and Oriental rabbis of North Africa and the Levant, the winds of change blowing from the West brought about transformations that were for the better as well as for the worse. But they were not the whirlwind that swept through the palace of Rabbi Naḥman's parable.

---

[32] See Bernard Lewis, *The Shaping of the Modern Middle East* (Oxford University Press: New York and Oxford, 1994), pp. 105–110; Michael Youssef, *Revolt Against Modernity: Muslim Zealots and the West* (E. J. Brill: Leiden, 1985), pp. 53–57 *et passim;* William Montgomery Watt, *Islamic Fundamentalism and Modernity* (Routledge: London and New York, 1988), pp. 51–53 *et passim.*

TWO

Modernist Traditionalists — Elijah Bekhor Ḥazzan & Raphael Aaron Ben Simeon: Their Thought and *Oeuvre*

Among the many rabbinical figures of Sephardi and Oriental Jewry during the early years of transition into modern times, two individuals stand out for the quality of their leadership, their intellect, and their legal and literary legacy — Raphael Aaron Ben Simeon and Elijah Bekhor Ḥazzan.[1] They were born in the same year, 5608 according to the Jewish calendar (1847/48), at opposite ends of the Oriental Jewish world — Ben Simeon in Rabat, on the Atlantic coast of Morocco, and Ḥazzan in Izmir, on the Aegean coast of Turkey. Both were scions of distinguished Sephardi rabbinical families. Both spent their formative years in Jerusalem, where Ben Simeon's father was head of the Moghrabi Jewish community and Ḥazzan's grandfather was the Rishon le-Ṣiyyon (Sephardi Chief Rabbi of Palestine). In addition to their excellent Judaic educations, both young men studied several foreign languages including French, Spanish, Italian, and Arabic, and read widely in them. They also read the modern Hebrew press and literature. Elijah Ḥazzan even contributed a number of

---

[1] There are good biographical sketches of each of these men in Zvi Zohar, *Halakha u-Modernizaṣiyya: Darkhe Heʿanut Ḥakhme Miṣrayim le-Etgare ha-Modernizaṣiyya, 1822–1882* (Makhon Shalom Hartmann: Jerusalem, 1982), pp. 177–190. See also the briefer notices in Arieh Leib Frumkin, *Toledot Ḥakhme Yerushalayim Mi-Shnat H"A R"N la-Yeṣira ʿad H"A TR"L la-Yeṣira,* with notes and additions by Eliezer Rivlin (Defus Solomon: Jerusalem, 1928–1930), vol. 3, pp. 306 and 307–308.

articles to the Prussian Hebrew newspaper *Ha-Maggid*. The Sephardi intellectual Abraham Elmaleh notes in his obituary of Raphael Aaron Ben Simeon that he had an impressive knowledge of modern Hebrew literature. Both rose rapidly in Jerusalem's rabbinical circles, and each of them served as secretary to the *bet din* (law court) of their respective communities.

Both men had the opportunity to travel abroad for extended periods of time as *sheluḥe de rabbanan* (rabbinical emissaries for the religious institutions of the Holy Land). Elijah Ḥazzan went to England, France, and Italy in 1870, where he met, among others, Sir Moses Montefiore and Baron de Rothschild. Two years later he went on an extended mission to Tunisia and Algeria, where he stayed until 1874. The young rabbi was deeply impressed by what he had seen in Europe and by the impact of modern civilization on its emancipated Jewry. He was also impressed and concerned by the radical transformation that was taking place among Jews in North Africa, particularly in French Algeria. He gave voice to his thoughts about what he had observed in a philosophical dialogue entitled *Zikhron Yerushalayim* (Remembrance of Jerusalem) which he published in Livorno in 1874 on his way back to Palestine at the press of the Sephardi intellectual Elijah Benamozegh.[2]

The scene of the dramatic dialogue is set in the home of a wealthy Jew in Tunis in which a young Palestinian rabbi, who is of a leading Sephardi family, but who chooses not to reveal his name, is a guest. Over the course of sixteen days, the host and his family, several visitors, and the rabbi discuss a wide range of topics on Jewish theology, law, and society, with each of the interlocutors representing different points of view. Through his

[2] Concerning him, see the brief account Marc D. Angel, *Voices in Exile: A Study in Sephardic Intellectual History* (Ktav Publishing House: Hoboken, New Jersey, 1991), pp. 155–157 et passim. For a detailed biography, see Guglielmo Lattes, *Vita e opere di Elia Benamozegh: Cenni, Considerazioni, Notes con Ritratto dell' Illustre Rabbino* (Stab. Tip. S. Belforte e.c.: Livorno, 1901).

Plate 3 Rabbi Raphael Aaron Ben Simeon (1847–1928), Sephardi intellectual, halakhic authority, who was Chief Rabbi of Cairo, 1881–1921.

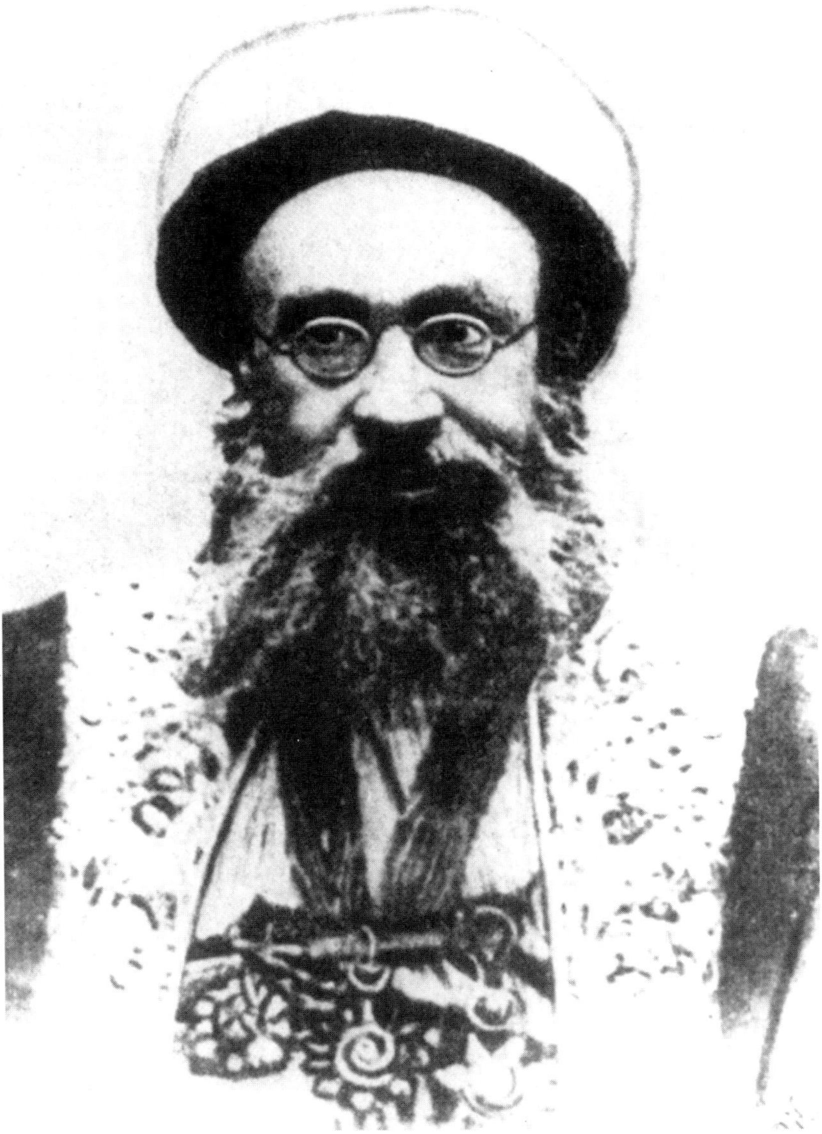

Plate 4 Rabbi Elijah Bekhor Ḥazzan (1847–1908), a leading Sephardi intellectual and halakhic authority, who was Chief Rabbi of Alexandria, 1878–1908.

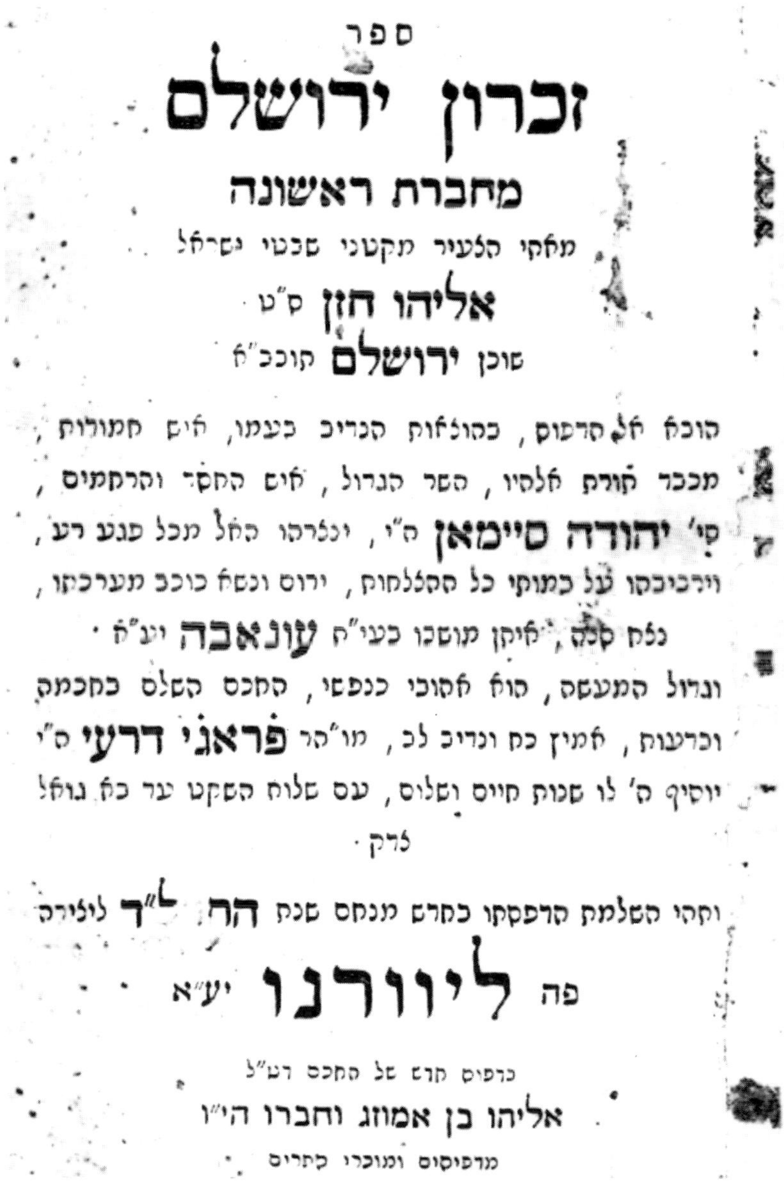

ספר

זכרון ירושלם

מחברת ראשונה

מאתי הצעיר מקטני שבטי ישראל

אליהו חזן ס"ט

שוכן ירושלם תוככ"א

הובא אל הדפוס, בהוצאות הנדיב בעמו, איש חמודות,
מכבד תורת אלהיו, השר הגדול, איש החסד והרחמים,
כ' יהודה סיימאן ה"י, ינצרהו האל מכל פגע רע,
וירכיבהו על במותי כל הצלחות, ירום ונשא כוכב מערכתו,
נצח סלה, איתן מושבו בעי"ת עונאבה יע"א ·
וגדול המעשה, הוא אחוהי כנפשי, החכם השלם בחכמה
ובדעות, אמיץ כח ונדיב לב, מו"הר פראג'י דרעי ס"ט
יוסיף ה' לו שנות חיים ושלום, עם שלות השקט עד בא גואל
לצדק ·

ויהי השלמת הדפסתו בחדש מנחם שנת התרל"ד ליצירה

פה ליוורנו יע"א

בדפוס חדש של החכם רע"ל

אליהו בן אמוזג וחברו הי"ו

מדפיסים ומוכרי ספרים

Plate 5 Title page of Elijah Ḥazzan's philosophical dialogue *Zikhron Yerushalayim* (1874).

characters, who include communal officials, rabbis, and a number of European Jews, Elijah Ḥazzan demonstrates his own familiarity with the wide spectrum of opinions and perspectives current in the Jewish world of his day. What is remarkable about the dialogue is that he is able to present opinions which he himself did not share with a considerable degree of fairness and dispassion. The mysterious young rabbi, who will only identity himself as *ha-ger* (the "stranger"), is, of course, the voice of the author himself. In *Zikhron Yerushalayim*, Elijah Ḥazzan makes it clear that he believes that modernity is for better or for worse an irreversible, worldwide phenomenon which sooner or later will touch every Jewish community. In order to respond effectively to the challenges of the new age, Jews must convene an assembly in which all of the diverse currents of contemporary Jewry are represented. In fact, such an assembly is actually convened in the book by a very exalted and distinguished leader who is identified only as *ha-Nasi* ("the President").[3]

An important subtheme that runs throughout the book, and is alluded to in the title, is the love of Zion. The author implies that this intensely deep sentiment which is shared by most Jews can be a force for the unification of the diverse currents of modern Jewry. Although Rabbi Ḥazzan's traditional proto-Zionism has none of the highly developed programmatic qualities of his much older contemporary, Rabbi Judah Alkalai (see Chapter Three), it was part of a wider revival within Sephardi Jewry during this period.

Raphael Aaron Ben Simeon also went abroad as a *shadar* a decade later in 1885. His mission took him across North Africa. On his journey, he even met briefly his friend and peer Elijah Ḥazzan in Tripoli.

As a scholarly *maskil*, Ben Simeon had a personal interest in the discovery and publication of Jewish manuscripts, and he had

---

[3] More than half the book is devoted to this assembly. See Elijah Ḥazzan, *Zikhron Yerushalayim* (Elijah Benamozegh: Livorno, 1874), pp. 48–117.

hoped to find such treasures while in Fez, which had been one of the early havens for exiles fleeing Spain. He did indeed find chests filled with manuscripts that were being allowed by their keepers to rot and crumble. He also discovered that the venerable Castilian congregation in Fez possessed only a single crumbling manuscript of its ancient liturgy which was used by the cantor while the rest of the congregation prayed from memory or listened passively. He attributed this sorry state of affairs not to any fault on the part of the Moroccan Jews, but to their lack of enlightenment. "It would be wrong to blame them for not publishing such treasures," he writes.

> Indeed what were they to do? For the art of printing is not a common sight in any of the cities of Morocco. And it seems like something wondrous and supernatural in the eyes of many of our brethren there who have never gone outside the boundaries of their hometowns or taken a step beyond. They have no idea about all that is taking place in the world, with the exception of a very few well-informed and knowledgeable individuals who have visited the cities of Europe and elsewhere, where the light of the Enlightenment shines.[4]

Ben Simeon succeeded in convincing another Fasi congregation, that of the ancient *Toshavim*, the indigenous community dating back prior to the arrival of the Sephardim, to let him publish their prayerbook in Jerusalem in 1889 under the title of *Ahavat ha-Qadmonim*. The Moroccan Jews were so pleased with the printed *siddur*, that they acquiesced to Ben Simeon's suggestion during his second visit to the country in 1889/90 that they establish a learned society dedicated to the propagation of the Moroccan and Sephardi intellectual heritage through the publication of works in manuscript. Such societies had been established in Europe in the wake of the Haskala, the most famous being the Mekize Nirdamim Society ("Rousers of Those Who Slumber") founded in 1862. The new society was called

---

[4] Editor's introduction to Jacob Aben Ṣur, *Mishpaṭ u-Ṣdaqa be-Ya'aqov*, vol. 1 (Alexandria: Farag Ḥayyim Mizraḥi, 1894), p. 2. See also his introduction to the prayerbook *Ahavat ha-Qadmonim:* (Jerusalem: Samuel ha-Levi Zuckerman, 1889).

Doveve Sifte Yeshenim ("Those Who Give Speech to Sleepers' Lips"), clearly taking its inspiration from its European predecessor.[5]

Both of the young rabbis from Jerusalem had gained reputations during their missions abroad as *sheluḥe de rabbanan* not only as scholars, but as forward-looking individuals, endowed with the qualities of leadership. Even at this early stage in their respective careers, they demonstrated a definite inclination toward the moderate wing of the *Haskala*. Shortly after the conclusion of their respective missions — in another striking parallel in the course of their lives — each was appointed by the Ottoman Government as a ḥakham bashi, a position which in the Tanzimat era was often reserved for reform-minded men who were considered sympathetic to the progressivist ideals being espoused in Istanbul.[6]

In 1874, Elijah Ḥazzan took office in Tripoli as the first imperial chief rabbi of the province of Tripolitania. Within a year after his arrival, he set about modernizing the traditional education by introducing instruction in Arabic, Italian (which was the European language of commerce in Libya), mathematics, and vocational skills into the community-run talmud torah schools. He also wanted to establish a new, single, consolidated community school with individual classrooms. His educational reforms ran up against strong opposition from local conservative elements, whom the contemporary chronicler, Mordechai ha-Kohen, himself an ardent supporter of Rabbi Ḥazzan, refers to as

---

[5] Ben Simeon gives an account of the founding of the Doveve Sifte Yeshenim in his introduction to the collected responsa of Rabbi Jacob Aben Ṣur, *Mishpat u-Ṣdaqa be-Ya'aqov* (Alexandria: Farag Ḥayyim Mizraḥi, 1894), p. 2. Concerning Mekiẓe Nirdamim, which by the way still exists, see Israel Ta-Shma, "Mekiẓe Nirdamim," *Encyclopaedia Judaica*, XI, cols. 1270–1271.

[6] Concerning the development of the Ottoman chief rabbinate in this period, see H. Z. [J. W.] Hirschberg,"The Oriental Jewish Communities," in *Religion in the Middle East: Three Religions in Concord and Conflict*, vol. 1, ed. A. J. Arberry (Cambridge University Press: Cambridge, 1969), pp. 196–202; and Stillman, *The Jews of Arab Lands in Modern Times*, pp. 10–11.

"the juridical party" (*ᶜadat ha-dayyanim*).[7] The opposition objected to the introduction of foreign languages into Jewish schools because it would disseminate heresy. The chief rabbi responded to his critics in a lengthy responsum in which he argued that the study of foreign languages, far from being forbidden by the halakha, was on the contrary, approved by it. Among the numerous proofs that he marshals is the fact that the members of the Sanhedrin of old were required to know many foreign languages in order to be able to hear evidence directly without the medium of a translator. Furthermore, he argues, the study of the sciences and other forms of Gentile wisdom "pose no danger to those whose spirit is sound, but only to those whose hearts are already stained with turbidity as was the case with Elisha Aḥer [i.e., the apostate *tanna* Elisha Ben Abuya]."[8] Rabbi Ḥazzan received support for his views from some of the leading Sephardi rabbinical figures of the day in the Holy Land, in Tunis, and Turkey.[9]

During the fourteen years of his tenure in Tripoli, Rabbi Ḥazzan labored for progressive reforms within the context of the traditional religious and communal framework. At the same time, he was able to steer a course between the reactionary elements and the more Europeanized radical modernizers. And true to the

[7] Mordekhai ha-Kohen, *Higgid Mordecai: Histoire de la Libye et de ses Juifs, lieux d'habitation et coutumes,* ed. Harvey E. Goldberg (Institut Ben-Zvi: Jerusalem, 1978), p. 236 [Hebrew]. See also Yehuda Kahalon, "ha-Maᶜavaq ᶜal Demutah ha-Ruḥanit shel ha-ᶜEda ha-Yehudit be-Luv ba-Me'a ha-19 uva-ᶜAsor ha-Rishon shel ha Me'a ha-ᶜEsrim," in *Zakhor Le-Abraham: Mélanges Abraham Elmaleh à l'occasion du cinquième anniversaire de sa mort (21 Adar II 5727),* ed. H. Z. Hirschberg (Comité de la Communauté Marocaine: Jerusalem, 1972), pp. 85–86 and 92–94.

[8] Ḥazzan, *Taᶜalumot Lev*, vol. 1 (Elijah Benamozegh: Livorno, 1879), pp. 14a–16b. (The quotation is found on p. 15b).

[9] Their letters are appended to his responsum, ibid., pp. 17a–18a. The rabbis were Abraham Ashkenazi, the Rishon le-Ṣiyyon in Palestine, Abraham Haggege and Abraham Boccara, the chief rabbis of the Twansa and the Grana communities of Tunis, and Abraham Palache, the ḥakham bashi of Izmir.

role of the many a Sephardi *ḥakham*, he successfully endeavored to prevent these polar forces from tearing the communal fabric asunder.

In 1878, Elijah Ḥazzan was called to Alexandria to take up the position of ḥakham bashi there. Three years later, his friend Raphael Aaron Ben Simeon became chief rabbi in Cairo. Over the next two decades, they worked as close colleagues in what was at that time the most rapidly developing country in the Middle East. It was during this period, as spiritual leaders of Egyptian Jewry, that they produced an impressive and rather remarkable body of halakhic work which has formed the core of two separate academic studies produced in Israel — one by Yehuda Nini and the other by Zvi Zohar.[10]

What is most striking about the outlook of Ḥazzan and Ben Simeon is not their generally tolerant approach in dealing with halakhic issues that arose in the wake of the changes taking place in both general and Jewish society. There are many parallels that may be found in the legal decisions of other Eastern rabbis of the period. Nor is it the boldness of some of their actions. Rather, what is most striking is their clear comprehension that the modern era was a time of fundamental change, that it provided a totally unprecedented existential situation that required creative Jewish responses, and that it was not a temporary phenomenon that had merely to be waited out. Not all Middle Eastern rabbis grasped this fact, or at least not as clearly. In examining the decisions of nineteenth and early twentieth century Iraqi *poseqim* such as ᶜAbd Allah Somekh and Joseph Ḥayyim, the Israeli anthropologist Shlomo Deshen opines that even as these sages confronted new problems resulting from technological and social change, they appear to have been

---

[10] Yehuda Nini, *Mi-Mizraḥ umi-Yam: Yehude Miṣrayim, Ḥayye Yom Yom ve-Hishtaqfutam be-Sifrut ha-Shut, 5642–5674* (Tel Aviv University: Tel: Aviv, 1979/80); Zvi Zohar, *Halakha u-Modernizaṣiyya: Darkhe Heᶜanut Ḥakhme Miṣrayim le-Etgare ha-Modernizaṣiyya, 1822–1882* (Makhon Shalom Hartmann: Jerusalem, 1982).

"unaware ... of the sociocultural ramifications of the problem at hand, unaware of changing times."[11]

Our two Egyptian rabbis, by contrast, were acutely aware of religious implications of modernity. They understood — and emphasized — that one of the most significant new realities that it brought was a hitherto unparalleled measure of freedom of choice to the individual. Rabbi Raphael Aaron Ben Simeon writes in one of his responsa:

> It was unheard of in any previous time that the governing authorities would loosen restraints so that an individual would be free in his religion and belief to the point that no one can say to him, "What doest thou?" No one has the authority to chastise a person who commits a religious transgression, even if it is committed in public. This is the result of the freedom and liberty [*ha ḥofesh veha deror*] prevailing in the land.[12]

In another case, he writes, "It is not in our power to eradicate [objectionable practices such as prostitution by Jewish women] because of the prevailing freedom and liberty [again, *ha-ḥofesh veha-deror*]." His colleague, Elijah Ḥazzan uses the same phrase ("freedom and liberty") in his writings as well. This intellectual grasp of the centrality of the phenomenon of individual freedom accords precisely with the sociologist Peter Berger's definition of modernization as "a shift from giveness to choice on the level of meaning."[13]

[11] Shlomo Deshen, "Baghdad Jewry in Late Ottomon Times: The Emergence of Social Classes and of Secularization," *AJS Review* 19:1 (1994), p. 38.

[12] Raphael Aaron Ben Simeon, *Umi-Ṣur Devash* (Samuel ha-Levi Zuckerman: Jerusalem, 1911/12), p. 111b.

[13] Raphael Aaron Ben Simeon, *Nehar Miṣrayim* (Farag Ḥayyim Mizraḥi: Alexandria, 1907/08), p. 100a; Elijah Ḥazzan, *Ta'alumot Lev*, vol 4 (Farag Ḥayyim Mizraḥi: Alexandria, 1907), p. 45a; Peter L. Berger, *Pyramids of Sacrifice* (Basic Books: New York, 1976), p. 186. It is important to note that for many Muslim writers in the nineteenth century, words like *ḥuriyya* ("liberty") were often perceived as meaning "libertinism." The question of liberty versus authority has been one of the central issues of modern social thought. As Eisenstadt has observed, "Modern social order was conceived as one in which the scope of liberty was continuously extended, thus necessarily creating the problem of maintenance of stability and order in the face of expanding areas of liberty." S. N. Eisenstadt, *Tradition, Change, and Modernity* (Robert E. Krieger Publishing: Malabar, Florida, 1983), p. 4.

The new freedom had positive was well as negative consequences, particularly on the collective level. Jews could now perform certain religious rites in public, such as a holding a joyful daytime procession to bring a new Torah scroll into the synagogue. Such public displays by non-Muslims were traditionally forbidden under Islamic law. "But now, thank God," writes Raphael Aaron Ben Simeon, "that freedom and liberty prevail in the land ... it is no longer correct to follow the previous practice of bringing the Torah scroll furtively in the dead of night."[14]

While recognizing the new existential reality of personal freedom of the individual, Rabbis Ben Simeon and Ḥazzan also believed that there was an important role for rabbis in the new order of things. They felt that in working for the spiritual good of the community, they could not overreact to all of the changes that were taking place with ever-stricter and more unrealistic demands. "The present age is not prepared for the addition of new prohibitions not instituted by the early sages," observes Elijah Ḥazzan. His colleague Ben Simeon shared these sentiments. The rabbi as spiritual teacher and jurist must "exert himself for the communal good and for the maintenance of its purity by every means that presents itself without pulling the cord of stringency to its limit."[15] These sentiments stand in strong contrast to the stance of most Ashkenazic rabbinic authorities who, to this day, continually institute newer and more demanding legal strictures (*ḥumrot*).

An important corollary to this approach was their application of the talmudic notion of *ḥuqqat ha-goy* ("Gentile custom"). Although the *halakha* distinguishes between forbidden Gentile practices connected with ritual or immorality and those which are of a neutral character, Ashkenazi rabbis since the Middle Ages had tended to cite the principle of *ḥuqqat ha-goy* to prohibit any emulation of non-Jews. During the nineteenth century, many Eastern European Orthodox rabbis had objected

[14] Ben Simeon, *Nehar Miṣrayim*, p. 118b.

[15] Ḥazzan, *Ta'alumot Lev*, vol. 3, p. 59a; Ben Simeon, *Umi-Ṣur Devash*, p. 111a.

to Jews wearing modern clothing because it was "Gentile practice," and many of the ceremonial innovations of Reform Judaism were rejected on these same grounds.[16] Sephardi rabbis, in contrast, had historically been more open to general culture and willing to look beyond the proverbial "four cubits of the law." And so it was with our two chief rabbis in Egypt.

In one case concerning the question of holding a wedding in the synagogue — and on Sunday — Elijah Ḥazzan specifically rejects the argument that this is forbidden because it is "Gentile practice." Traditionally, Jewish weddings were celebrated in a courtyard in the open air. However, due to the increase of modern wedding celebrations with mixed dancing and women in revealing evening dress, the rabbis of Egypt had decided to make an ordinance requiring weddings to be held in the synagogue as a way of maintaining greater modesty and decorum. When one of the leaders of the congregation in Alexandria informed the Ḥakham Bashi that he had been told by an Ashkenazi rabbi that this was forbidden, as was in addition holding a wedding there on Sunday, because it was "Gentile practice," Elijah Ḥazzan issued a responsum specifically rejecting such an argument. After reviewing the halakhic literature, he concludes that, if as he has shown, holding weddings in the synagogue, and on Sunday, is clearly permitted by the Talmud, and that those who forbade it in later ages did so for reasons pertinent to their specific time and place, "why should we come and issue a ban on the principle of Gentile practice?" He goes on to say that "one should not add on the basis of mere presumption to those things which the sages, who possessed the direct tradition from Sinai, had designated as 'Gentile practices.' For if we were to forbid everything that had arisen first among the Christians and Muslims, we would be forbidding some permitted things as well."[17]

---

[16] Concerning "Gentile practice," see Meir Ydit, "Ḥukkat ha-Goi," *Encyclopaedia Judaica*, vol. 8, cols. 1061–1062.

[17] Elijah "Ḥazzan, Taʿalumot Lev, vol. 3, pp. 58a–59a (the quotations are from p. 59a).

Both Raphael Aaron Ben Simeon and Elijah Ḥazzan were prepared to take bold, even radical action when they believed it was warranted. Certainly the most salient example of this strong, halakhic activism is an instance in which the two men acted in concert and were able to bring the other rabbis of Egypt along with them.

In 1901, Rabbis Ben Simeon and Ḥazzan, together with their colleague Aaron Mendel ha-Kohen, the Chief Rabbi of Cairo's Ashkenazi community, issued an ordinance (*taqqana*) for all of Egypt, not merely forbidding, but annulling *ex post facto* all marriages that did not meet the following three criteria: (a) permission from the head of the rabbinical court, (b) the presence of at least a minyan (quorum of ten adult Jewish males) that included a representative of the rabbinical court, and (c) the signing of a marriage contract.

This unprecedented decree was issued in response to a problem that had reached critical proportions in the late nineteenth and early twentieth centuries. Egypt was a country of tremendous immigration at this time. The number of Jews in the country multiplied several times over during the second half of the nineteenth century. Between 1897 and 1907 alone, the Jewish population had risen from 25,000 to more than 38,000. The newcomers included both Ashkenazim and Sephardim. Among them, there was a high proportion of bachelors. Many young men entered into liaisons with Egyptian Jewish girls. Apparently, a common way to win the young woman's compliance was to perform a private marriage (something that is technically valid under Jewish law) before two friends acting as witnesses, promising to have a public ceremony at some future date. Later, when they had tired of the affair, the young men would simply abandon the young women, who were not only sadder and wiser, but also halakhically *ʿagunot,* women who could never remarry unless their husband were to die or grant them a writ of divorce. If not freed from their first marriage, any children they might bear by another man in the future would be considered illegitimate (*mamzerim*) with all of the serious disabilities that

that status entails. By dissolving all private marriages after the fact, the rabbis of Egypt, led by Ben Simeon, provided a bold solution to a religious problem and a social crisis.[18]

It is significant that Rabbis Ben Simeon and Ḥazzan achieved universal acceptance of the ordinance throughout the country, including the acceptance of the Ashkenazi community. Indeed, it was the only such nationwide ordinance in the modern era, and apparently it was a complete success. Although Jewish authorities generally, both Ashkenazi and Sephardi, seek to be lenient in whatever way they can when trying to solve problems involving *ᶜagunot* and *mamzerim*, Ashkenazi jurists did not allow such sweeping legislative action as that taken in Egypt. In the view of the European rabbis, each case had to be handled individually. They held to the opinion of Rabbi Moses Isserles (the Rama) in his gloss to the *Shulḥan ᶜArukh* that no public ordinance had the power to dissolve a marriage after the fact.[19]

As Louis Jacobs has observed, Sephardi rabbis were historically "bolder in their efforts to introduce new legislation in the sphere of marriage law in order to cope with the problem of the *ᶜagunah* ... or the widow bound to the levir (Deut. 25:5–10) who refuses ... to release her to marry another."[20] He attributes this

[18] The background to the ordinance, the legal reasoning behind it, and the text of the *taqqana* (Ben Simeon calls it a *haskama*, "agreement") itself are given in Raphael Aaron Ben Simeon, *Umi-Ṣur Devash*, 104b–113a; see also his *Nehar Miṣrayim*, vol. 2, pp. 170b–178a, where the Arabic text of the ordinance is also given and the process of its acceptance throughout Egypt is documented. For a discussion of the significance of this particular ruling and the theoretical basic basis behind it, see Zvi Zohar, "The Halakhic Teaching of Egyptian Rabbis in Modern Times, "*Peᶜamim* 16 (1983), pp. 65–88 [in Hebrew]; also idem, *Halaka u-Modernizaṣiyya*, pp. 126–143.

[19] See Abraham Haim Freimann, *Seder Qiddushin u-Nesu' in Aḥare Ḥatimat ha-Talmud* (Mossad Ha-Rav Kook: Jerusalem, 1964), pp. 322–323. By the way, Rabbi Menahem Mendel ha-Kohen's close ties to Sephardi community eventually resulted in his ouster by the Ashkenazi community as its chief rabbi in 1910. His colleague Ben Simeon immediately appointed him to the Sephardi rabbinic court.

[20] Louis Jacobs, "The Responsa of Rabbi Joseph Ḥayyim of Baghdad," in *Perspectives on Jews and Judaism: Essays in Honor of Wolfe Kelman*, ed. Arthur A. Chiel (The Rabbinical Assembly: New York, 1978), p. 195.

resolve to the Sephardi jurists' "complete autonomy" in administering family law, an autonomy that was not enjoyed by their Ashkenazi confreres in Europe. Certainly the action of the Egyptian rabbis was of apiece with this historical tradition. But it was more than that. It was also part and parcel of a positivist, activist stance vis-à-vis the problems and challenges arising with modern times. In Egypt, the rabbis no longer enjoyed total autonomy, and as we have already noted, were well aware of the limitations on the powers of coercion and communal discipline due to the existential freedom of the individual that came with modernity. Indeed, they were impelled to take this bold action because so many of the immigrant young men involved were foreign subjects who, under the so-called Capitulation Agreements (Arabic, *imtiyazat*), were not under either Egyptian or their jurisdiction.

Two years after the promulgation of the marriage ordinance, Rabbi Elijah Ḥazzan helped to organize and took a leading part in an international rabbinical conference in Cracow. The conference was the brain child of his Ashkenazi colleague from Cairo, Rabbi Aaron Mendel ha-Kohen. Many of the issues it took up were the very ones that Elijah Ḥazzan had advocated for such an assembly years earlier in his philosophical dialogue *Zikhron Yerushalayim*. Rabbi Ḥazzan was elected honorary president of the conference. One issue which he insisted the conference deal with forcefully was the recrudescence of the blood libel in modern times. This medieval accusation was rife in Eastern Europe at this time and had been introduced into the Levant, including Egypt, by Christian missionaries and French intellectual antisemites. Not only did he and other notable figures denounce the pernicious accusation, but at his insistence, the delegates of the conference with government dignitaries in attendance held a solemn ceremony before the open ark in the synagogue stating upon oath that no Jew anywhere had ever committed such an act. Although there had been some opposition to the need for such a ceremony, Rabbi Ḥazzan prevailed, countering that he himself had met cultured Gentiles who believed the blood libel and that such a well-publicized act would make a strong impression on the educated and perhaps on the uneducated as well. He obviously appreciated the effectiveness of public relations using the modern media.[21]

Following the death of the Ḥakham Jacob Saul Elyachar in 1906, Rabbi Ḥazzan was invited to come to Jerusalem to take up the position of Rishon le-Ṣiyyon, the chief rabbi of the Holy Land, the post — it will be recalled — that was once held by his grandfather. He declined, however, in spite of his deep sentiments for the Land of Israel, not wishing to be involved in the often fractious politics of the Yishuv. He remained in Alexandria as ḥakham bashi until his death two years later in June 1908, at the age of sixty or sixty-one. He had just published the fourth and final volume of his collected responsa *Taʿalumot Lev*, the preceding year. He was still remembered with the deepest affection and veneration by Alexandrian Jewry decades later.

Rabbi Raphael Aaron Ben Simeon outlived his friend and colleague by a decade and a half. During that period, he continued to provide strong and effective leadership for Cairene and Egyptian Jewry. He also continued to produce an impressive output of halakhic and literary works including a historical and biographical dictionary of the Egyptian rabbinate, *Ṭuv Misrayim* [*Egypt's Goodness*], a volume of his collected responsa, *Umi-Ṣur Devash* [*Honey from the Rock*], and numerous other books and treatises.[22] He was held in high regard by Jews and non-Jews alike. The Coptic writer, Shahin Makariyus describes him as

---

[21] Elijah Ḥazzan, *Taʿalumot Lev*, vol. 4, pp. 45a–47b. His role in the conference is also discussed by Marc D. Angel, *Voices in Exile: A Study in Sephardic Intellectual History* (Ktav Publishing House: Hoboken, 1991), pp. 198–200; and Jacob Landau, *Jews in Nineteenth-Century Egypt* (New York University Press and University of London Press: New York and London, 1969), p. 99. The most extensive details of the conference, including a list of the more than 300 participants, the issues discussed, and the resolutions adopted, are to be found in Aaron Mendel ha-Kohen, *Yad Re"em*, ed. Ḥayyim Naphtali Weisblum (n.p.: Tel Aviv, 1959/60), Part I, pp. 3–79.

[22] Raphael Aaron Ben Simeon, *Ṭuv Miṣrayim* (Defus ha-Rav Samuel ha-Levi Zuckerman: Jerusalem, 1908).

Gentle of character, affable of demeanor, well-versed in tradition, modest in both word and deed. His attributes include love of one's neighbor, establishing harmony between people, as well as other praiseworthy things.[23]

It was a mark of Ben Simeon's character that when his friend Aaron Mendel ha-Kohen was removed from his office as chief rabbi of the Ashkenazi community of Egypt, he immediately appointed him to a fulltime, salaried position on the Sephardi *bet din* (rabbinical court), a most extraordinary act to be sure. In fact, both Raphael Aaron Ben Simeon and Aaron Mendel ha-Kohen had always worked to break down the barriers between the two communities. (Ha-Kohen's closeness to the Sephardim was probably one of the reasons for his dismissal.)[24]

Rabbi Ben Simeon resigned from his own post in 1921 after thirty years in office expressing a desire to make ᶜaliyah, although the Egyptian writer Maurice Fargeon suggests that he made his decision following "a misunderstanding" with the Community Council. It is perhaps a mark of the forward-looking spirit of the man that he chose to settle in the recently founded Jewish city of Tel Aviv, the very heart of the New *Yishuv*, rather than in Jerusalem, the center of the Old Yishuv, where he had been raised. He was, however, buried in the Holy City when he died in October 1928.[25]

The lives and careers of Rabbis Elijah Ḥazzan and Raphael Aaron Ben Simeon spanned much of the crucial period when Oriental Jewry had its formative encounter with modernity. They were both born, raised, and educated in premodern, traditional surroundings, and they remained thoroughly dedicated to traditional Judaism their entire lives and worked with the juridical and communal framework of the *Halakha*. Like many

[23] Shahin Makariyus, *Ta'rikh al-Isra'iliyyin* (Maṭbaᶜat al-Muqtaṭaf: Cairo, 1904), p. 209.

[24] Ḥayyim Naphtali Weisblum, "Toledot ha-Meḥabber," in Aaron Mendel ha-Kohen, *Yad Re"em*, p. 13; also Zohar, *Halakha u-Modernizaṣiyya*, pp. 198–199.

[25] Maurice Fargeon, *Les Juifs en Egypte depuis les origines jusqu'à ce jour: histoire générale suivie d'un aperçu documentaire* (Imprimerie Paul Barbey: Cairo, 1938), p. 201.

of their Sephardi and Oriental rabbinical counterparts, they responded to the challenges of the modern era in the classic Sephardi tradition of *poseqim* (decisors) with a sang-froid and a boldness that was rarely shown by the early Ashkenazi religious authorities when European Jewry was first drawn into the tempestuous modern world. They also were squarely in the Sephardi tradition of tolerance and working for the preservation of communal unity in contradistinction to German neo-Orthodoxy which came to embrace certain positive aspects of general culture, but generally sought to separate itself from non-observant Jews. Although Ḥazzan and Ben Simeon are representative in the scope of their communal work and in the thrust of their legal *oeuvre*, they are not completely typical of their fellow Sephardi rabbis either. For they perceived with perhaps greater clarity than any of the other individuals that we have discussed the very nature of modern times, its spirit, and its existential difference from what had existed before. They were cognizant of their limitations, but at the same time appear to have been convinced that they could effectively provide the entire Jewish community — and not only the fully observant — with meaningful religious guidance in the new age

THREE

"My Heart's in the East" — Sephardi Zionism

One of the distinguishing features — symptomatic ills, some might argue — of modern times is nationalism. This "peculiarly modern ideology"[1] evolved and spread throughout Europe following the French Revolution and eventually sprouted over much of the world. During the nineteenth and twentieth centuries, national movements have proliferated among many peoples, including the Jews. Zionism, or Jewish nationalism, was one response of the Jews to modernity. But unlike so many new currents and sentiments within Jewry, this one was not entirely borrowed from the Gentile world. Even in its most radical secularist form, it was rooted in two millennia of messianic hope for redemption.

The mainstream modern Zionist movement was born and developed among Ashkenazi Jewry in Europe. And the World Zionist Organization was founded and dominated by Central and Eastern European Jews. The majority of the *ḥalutzim* who built the new Yishuv and its institutions in Palestine were Ashkenazim, and it was they who became the principal founding fathers of the State of Israel. It is not surprising, therefore, that most of the standard histories of Zionism, such as those of

---

[1] Nationalism is also "a peculiarly Western construction." See the thought-provoking discussion in Peter L. Berger, Brigitte Berger, and Hansfried Kellner, *The Homeless Mind: Modernization and Consciousness* (Random House: New York, 1973), pp. 167–170.

Hertzberg, Laquer, and Vital,[2] pay virtually no attention to the evolution of Zionist thought and activity, whether religious or secular, among Sephardi and Oriental Jewry. The only Sephardi figure who usually receives some mention in these surveys is the Bosnian Rabbi Judah Alkalai, who was an important harbinger of religious Zionism and whose writings came to have some retrospective importance within the later movement.

Before modern times, some of the most articulate voices of the traditional Jewish longing for Zion had emanated from the Sephardi and Oriental Jewish world. Judah ha-Levi, the poet laureate of medieval Andalusian Jewry gave classic expression to this yearning in his sublime cycle of Hebrew verses known as the "Songs of Zion" and in his Judaeo-Arabic dialogue, *The Kuzari*. One of these poems that begins with verse "My heart's in the East, while I'm in the furthermost West/How can I taste what I eat and how can it please me?" became a theme song for later *ḥoveve Ṣiyyon* all the way up to the modern era. Ha-Levi, in fact, took his verses and his philosophical treatise seriously, and in

[2] Arthur Hertzberg, *The Zionist Idea* (Atheneum: New York, 1976); Walter Laquer, *A History of Zionism* (Holt, Rinehart and Winston: New York, 1972); David Vital, *Origins of Zionism* (Clarendon Press: Oxford, 1975). Over the past two decades there have been a number of studies, mostly produced in Israel, dealing with Zionism among Sephardi and Oriental Jewry. Most of this new body of research, is devoted to secular/political movement and not to the religious aspects of Zionism. A comprehensive, synthetic history of Sephardi Zionism still remains to be written. For a brief assessment of the scholarly work that has been done, see Michel Abitbol, "Research on Zionism and Aliya of Oriental Jewry — Methodological Aspects," *Pe'amim* 39 (1989), pp. 3–14 [in Hebrew].

Plate 6 Rabbi Judah Alkalai (1798–1878), Bosnian-born Sephardi harbinger of modern religious Zionism.

the twilight of his life set out for the Holy land, where he died in 1141.[3]

Thousands of Sephardim settled in Ottoman Palestine in the sixteenth century, and Jerusalem, Tiberias, and above all Safed became centers of their spiritual and economic activity. Sephardi courtiers at the Sublime Porte in Constantinople conceived bold projects for developing the Holy Land. Doña Gracia Mendes and her nephew Don Joseph Nasi undertook the rebuilding of Tiberias with a patent from Sultan Sulayman the Magnificent. The scheme to restore Tiberias had definite messianic overtones since there was a tradition that the Messiah would appear there. The plan also had a practical side. Even while he was still a nominal Christian in Italy, Don Joseph had proposed the idea of a Jewish commonwealth that would be a refuge for persecuted Jews.[4]

Throughout the succeeding centuries, Sephardi and Oriental Jewry maintained very strong, direct ties with the land of Israel to a much greater extent than did their brethren in Europe. This was due to the greater physical propinquity of most of North African and Levantine Jews to the Holy Land. It was also due to

---

[3] The best known "Songs of Zion" in the Hebrew original with accompanying English translations may be found in *Selected Poems of Jehudah Halevi*, ed. Heinrich Brody and trans. Nina Salaman (Philadelphia, 1924). The most complete translation of Ha-Levi's philosophical dialogue is *The Kuzari: An Argument for the Faith of Israel*, trans. Hartwig Hirschfeld (George Routledge & Sons: London, 1905). Some historians have doubted whether ha-Levi actually reached the Holy Land. However, on the basis of letters from the Cairo, Geniza, it is now certain that he at least reached the port of Tyre. See S. D. Goitein, "The Biography of Rabbi Judah ha-Levi in the Light of the Cairo Geniza Documents," *Proceedings of the American Academy for Jewish Research* 28 (1959), pp. 41–56.

[4] For a brief survey of this period, see Norman A. Stillman, *The Jews of Arab Lands: A History and Source Book* (Jewish Publication Society: Philadelphia, 1979), pp. 87–90. Concerning the scheme to restore Tiberias, see Cecil Roth, *The House of Nasi, The Duke of Naxos* (Jewish Publication Society: Philadelphia, 1948), pp. 97–135; and J. Braslavsky, "Jewish Settlement in Tiberias from Don Joseph Nasi to Ibn Yaish, "*Zion* 5:1 (1940), pp. 45–72 [in Hebrew]; also Stillman, ibid, pp. 293–294.

the fact that, until the colonial era, the vast majority of Oriental Jews lived in the Ottoman Empire, of which Palestine was a part. And even those who lived outside Ottoman territory in Morocco to the West, or in Persia and Central Asia to the East, still felt that their ancestral homeland was within the same Islamic world in which they lived. Many Jewish communities in that Islamic world had a long-standing practice of supporting institutions in the four holy cities of Jerusalem, Hebron, Safed, and Tiberias. The rabbinical emissaries (*sheluḥe de-rabbanan*, or *shadarim* for short), who frequently made the rounds of Middle Eastern and North African communities to collect contributions, were in fact important media of communication between the Palestinian Jewish community and the rest of Oriental Jewry. (It will be recalled that the two modernizing traditionalists that we discussed, Rabbi Elijah Ḥazzan and Rabbi Raphael Aaron Ben Simeon, were both rabbinical emissaries early in their careers.)

For centuries, there was an established tradition of ʿaliyah (literally, "ascent") to the Holy Land, particularly among North African Jews. This was, of course, a matter of individual personal piety, not a group phenomenon. There are numerous examples in Maghrebi responsa literature dealing the *miṣva* (religious duty) to settle the Land of Israel. I might also add that there are a considerable number of responsa that deal with cases of wives who do not wish to accompany their husbands on ʿaliyah because of the hazardous travel conditions. Seventeenth- and early eighteenth-century rabbis tended to accept the wife's argument and required the husband to pay his wife the money stipulated in her ketubba before departing. From the latter part of the eighteenth century, however, some authorities began to reject the wife's claim concerning the danger and permitted the husband to divorce her without payment. There are, by the way, even cases of wives who wish to go on ʿaliyah despite their husbands' objections. Because of the extremely great merit of the *miṣva* involved, the answer is invariably in the affirmative. Questions only arise as to whether the woman has the right to take her children with her, and if so, are there any restrictions as to their ages.[5]

The first half of the nineteenth century witnessed a dramatic increase in North African emigration to Palestine. Maghrebi Jews came to constitute a large, distinct community — the *Moghrabim*, or *ha-ᶜEda ha-Maᶜaravit* — in several towns, most notably Jerusalem, Haifa, and Jaffa. Indeed the revival of these towns in modern times was due in no small measure to this influx of settlers. Though impelled primarily by sentiments rooted in religious messianism, most of these North African and other Oriental Jewish immigrants were not engaged exclusively in prayer, study, and living the off the *ḥaluqqa* (the dole funded by charitable contributions from the Diaspora), but rather earned livelihoods through commerce, handicraft, and manual labor. This was in stark contrast to the majority of traditional Ashkenazi immigrants in the Holy Land prior to the Zionist pioneers who arrived during the last two decades of the nineteenth century. Sephardi and Oriental ᶜaliyah during the nineteenth century, I believe, while deeply traditional in many respects, was in part a response to modern currents that were just beginning to be felt during this period.

The emergence of cultural and political nationalism also had its impact on the thinking of some Sephardi rabbis. The earliest of these was Judah Bibas who was born in Gibraltar in 1780 into a noted Moroccan rabbinical family and received in addition to his religious training a secular education in Italy. For a time he headed a yeshiva in Gibraltar. In 1832, he took up the position of rabbi on the island of Corfu. Inspired by the Italian Risorgimento and the Greek uprising against the Turks, Bibas broke with the traditionalist quietist stance of waiting for the redemption and advocated a return of Jews to resettle their ancestral lands and to

---

[5] Numerous examples may be found in Eliezer Bashan, "ᶜAl Yaḥasam shel Ḥakhme Maroqo ba-Me'ot ha-XVIII-XIX le- Ḥovat ha-ᶜAliya le-Ereṣ Yisra'el," in *Yehude Ṣefon Afriqa ve-Ereṣ Yisra'el*, ed. Shalom Bar-Asher and Aharon Maman (Beyaḥad: Jerusalem, 1981), pp. 43–47.

wrest it by force if necessary. The most original element in his theology was his reinterpretation of the spiritual notion of *teshuva* (repentance) to its literal meaning, "return." That is, that Israel's redemption is not dependent exclusively upon its repentance (its return to God), but upon its physical return to the Holy Land. Bibas did not set down his ideas in writing, but preached them in Corfu and in the course of his travels in 1839 in the Ottoman and Austro-Hungarian Empires. It was during that year he met Rabbi Judah Alkalai, the ḥakham of Zemun in Croatia, and from the tone of the Balkan rabbi's occasional mention in his essays of what he heard from Bibas, it is clear that he made a profound impression upon him.[6]

Because of his extensive publications, it was Alkalai who became the best known Sephardi harbinger of Zionism. Unlike Bibas, the Bosnian-born Alkalai did not originally come to his proto-Zionism under the influence of modern nationalist ideas or even as a response to social and spiritual upheavals being experienced by European Jewry at that time. He began as a thoroughly traditional, pre-modern man. As Jacob Katz has convincingly shown in a careful analysis of Alkalai's writings, his thought processes were, in the beginning, exclusively those of the homiletic discourse of the Kabbala coupled with medieval philosophical speculation.[7] Alkalai's initial call for a return of Jews to their land was prompted by messianic calculations which

---

[6] Judah Alkalai, *Kitve ha-Rav Yehuda Alkalaʿi*, ed. Isaac Werfel (Mosad ha-Rav Kook: Jerusalem, 1944), vol. 1, pp. 21 and 27 (*Darkhe Noʿam*); pp. 208–209, 211–212 (*Minḥat Yehuda*); p. 243 (*Qol Qore'*). For the most recent light on Bibas's life and a good bibliography of the principal biographical studies devoted to him, see Arie Morgenstern, "Between Rabbi Yehuda Bibas and an Emissary of the Perushim in Jerusalem, "*Peʿamim* 40 (1989), pp. 156–159 [in Hebrew].

[7] Jacob Katz, "Meshiḥiyyut u-Le'umiyyut be-Mishnato shel ha-Rav Yehuda Alqalaʿi," in *Shivat Ṣiyyon: Me'assef le-Ḥeqer ha-Ṣiyyonut u-Tqumat Yisra'el,* vol. 4, eds. B. Dinur and Y. Heilprin (Ha-Sifriyya ha-Ṣiyyonit: Jerusalem, 1956), pp. 9–41. For a recent critical reassessment of Alkalai's life and of the studies (including Katz's) about him, see Jennie Lebel, "'Lovesick for Jerusalem' — Rabbi Yehuda Alkalai, the Political and Communal Context of His Activity," *Peʿamim* 40 (1989), pp. 21–48 [in Hebrew].

indicated that 1840 might be the year of Redemption or at least a major turning point toward that chiliastic moment. Events in the wider world were interpreted by him merely as heavenly signs. Over time, however, his thought did evolve in response to a growing and ever clearer awareness of the nature of change in the modern age.

The Damascus Blood Libel of 1840 was viewed by Alkalai as one of the aforementioned heavenly portents. But in his treatise *Minḥat Yehuda* (*Judah's Offering*), written shortly afterwards, it is clear that he is also impressed by the mission of Montefiore and Crémieux to the Levant on behalf of the Damascene Jews. The political power, influence, and energy of these men convinced him that they could turn to the rulers of the great nations and get them to grant freedom to Jews to return to their land as Cyrus the Great had done more than two millennia earlier. He had absorbed some of the optimism of Western European Jewry in its own ability to move events. His idea of convening an international congress of Jewish leaders fully empowered with the authority to make administrative decisions and to collect taxes for return and resettlement also seems to show some distant influence from contemporary Western models.[8] Other Sephardi religious leaders of the period had envisioned the need for a plenary assembly of representatives of world Jewry, as for example, Rabbi Elijah Bekhor Ḥazzan, whom we have already discussed.

While still remaining within his traditional categories of thought, Rabbi Alkalai increasingly begins to respond to specifically modern phenomena. In his little pamphlet *Qol Qore'* (*A Voice Crying Out*), Alkalai demonstrates his full awareness of the national and religious implications of the German Jewish Reform, even if he did not really understand the impetus behind it. He also for the first time senses that there is a major crisis in contemporary Judaism; namely that "the Children of Israel have

[8] *Kitve ha-Rav Yehuda Alqala'i*, pp. 195–196; ibid., pp. 179–182.

become two peoples — the new and the old."[9] At this stage of thinking, Alkalai identifies despair at the failure of messianic predictions as the cause of the Reform's defection from traditional Judaism, and Reform's defection as the cause for Jewish disunity.

During the 1850s Alkalai journeyed to England and western Europe hoping to garner support for his ideas, but with little success. The establishment of the Alliance Israélite Universelle in Paris in 1860 and the *Kolonisations-Verein für Palästina* in Frankfort-an-der-Oder that same year awakened in him new hope that the powerful Jews of the West were beginning to take the necessary steps toward national unity, on the one hand, and toward active resettlement of the land of Israel, on the other. Over the remaining two decades of his life, Alkalai's thought underwent a further evolution. His Zionism is still a religious Zionism, but it is increasingly imbued with contemporary nationalist sentiments. It is also permeated by a sense that this is a new period in human history as he eloquently proclaims in his essay *Nehamat ha-Areṣ* (*Consolation for the Land*) which he published in 1866:

> As Ezekiel (36:26) has prophesied, "I shall give you a new heart, and a new spirit will I place within you." The spirit of the times does not ask of the individual that he follow the arbitrariness of his heart, but rather that he seek the good of the collective. The spirit of the times has nothing to do with the Torah and divine service, for what the times require is without distinction of religion or people.... The spirit of the times demands freedom[10] and liberty for the success of the nation. And thus it demands of us to proclaim liberty to those in captivity.... The spirit of the times requires all of the countries to establish their land and to raise up their language. Likewise, it requires of us to establish our living home and to raise up our sacred language and to revive it.[11]

In this stirring passage, Rabbi Alkalai identifies Jewish national revival, not with a millenarian End of Days, but with a universal

---

9 *Kitve ha-Rav Yehuda Alqalaʿi*, vol. 1, pp. 239–258. The quotation is on p. 249.
10 Reading *ha-deror* instead of *ha-dor*.
11 *Kitve ha-Rav Yehuda Alqalaʿi*, vol. 2, p. 529.

phenomenon that is the right, indeed the duty, of all peoples everywhere. The national revival in his vision is tied to cultural revival. Hebrew is the one unifying language for the Jewish people. Alkalai's very first book, *Darkhe Noʿam* (*Ways of Pleasantness*), published in 1839 was a Ladino grammar of Hebrew. Although Alkalai himself only began to think in terms of an actual language revival for the Jewish people some years later. In his pamphlet *Meʿoded ʿAnavim* (*Encouraging the Humble*), he writes that "We must have a single spoken language in our holy land, and it is altogether fitting that the highest priority be given to our holy tongue."[12]

Alkalai was not the only Sephardi rabbi during the nineteenth century to feel the need for a Hebrew language revival. Israel Moses Ḥazzan, whom we mentioned before in connection with the question of foreign language education in Egypt published several appeals for Hebrew language study. In one of these, he points with admiration to the cultivation of classical Greek and Latin among Christians. Saul ha-Kohen of Tunis introduces his Hebrew grammar *Leḥem ha-Bikkurim* (*The Bread of the First Fruit Offering*) with the justification that other peoples are greatly interested in the study of their own language. And the Turkish rabbi Menahem Farḥi, justifies his Ladino-Hebrew grammar with the observation that other living languages are progressing. Throughout North Africa, rabbis were frequently to be found among the small circles of *maskilim* (members of the Haskala, or Jewish Enlightenment) who advocated a Hebrew language revival. They subscribed to Hebrew journals and read Hebrew books emanating from Europe and Palestine, as did laymen. In Mogador, on the southern coast of Morocco, Rabbi David Elqayim wrote poems in praise of the Hebrew language. In one of them, he calls upon the language to rise, awaken from its slumber, and to rejuvenate itself:

> Rise up, clear language of truth. Language of languages, why do you slumber? Return adorned to the days of your youth. Let your banner unfold and be not ashamed.

---

[12] *Kitve ha-Rav Yehuda Alqalaʿi*, vol. 2, p. 487.

Instead of being shut away in your lifetime, Be mightily exalted amidst your people.[13]

Judah Alkalai stands apart from all other Sephardi and Oriental rabbis for the intense, programmatic, and single-minded nature of his Zionism. However, there was far more sympathy for many of the sentiments he expressed among the rabbis of the East than among those of Ashkenaz. In fact, Alkalai came to view the European ultra-Orthodox leaders as being almost as guilty as the Reformers in causing division within Israel and delaying the Redemption. There was nothing in the Near East or North Africa comparable to the *Protestrabbiner* in Germany when the full-fledged Zionist movement came on the scene in the late nineteenth century.[14] There are two principal reasons for this striking

[13] Israel Moses Ḥazzan, *Words of Peace and Truth* (Samuel Meldola: London, 1845), pp. 13–14; Saul ha-Kohen, *Leḥem ha-Bikkurim* (Livorno, 1870); and Menahem Farḥi, Rav *Pe'alim* (Constantinople: Defus Avraham Shalto, 1880). For these and other examples of grammarians, see José Faur, "Early Zionist Ideals Among Sephardim in the Nineteenth Century," *Judaism* 25:1 (1976), pp. 56–60. For the Maghrebi haskala, see Joseph Chetrit, "New Consciousness of Anomaly and Language: The Beginnings of a Movement of Hebrew Enlightenment in Morocco at the End of the Nineteenth Century," *Miqqedem Umiyyam*, vol. 2, eds. Joseph Chetrit and Zvi Yehuda (University of Haifa Faculty of the Humanities: Haifa, 1986), pp. 129–168 [in Hebrew] (Elqayim's poem calling for the revival of Hebrew is on p. 145); idem., "Hebrew National Modernity against French Modernity: The Hebrew Haskalah in North Africa at the End of the Nineteenth Century," *Miqqedem Umiyyam*, vol. 3, ed. Joseph Chetrit (University of Haifa Faculty of the Humanities, 1990), pp. 11–78 [in Hebrew]; also Ephraim Ḥazan, "Language and Style in the Poetry of Rabbi David Kayyam," *Pe'amim* 17 (1983), pp. 53–75 [in Hebrew].

[14] Concerning the *Protestrabbiner*, see Getzel Kressel, "Protestrabbiner," *Encyclopaedia Judaica* 13, col. 1255; and Jehuda Reinharz, *Fatherland or Promised Land: The Dilemma of the German Jew, 1893–1914* (University of Michigan Press: Ann Arbor, 1975), pp. 172 and 174–176. In a highly tendentious article, the Tunisian historian Mohamed Larbi Snoussi tires to identify Rabbi Solomon Dana (1850–1913) as a North African *Protestrabbi* because according to an obituary notice "he was opposed to the politics of the Zionists, since he declared that the Messiah would come of his own accord and not through the politics of force or through war." See Mohammad Larbi Snoussi, "Aux origines du movement sioniste en Tunisie à la veilla de la grande guerre. Création de <<l'Aghoudat Sion>> et sa première scission (1887–1914), "*Les Cahiers de Tunisie* 44:3–4 (1991), p. 267. If Dana, who was the founder of the Ḥevrat Limmud ha-Talmud Yeshiva, had any strong theological reservations about political Zionism, he was not particularly outspoken about them.

contrast. First, Sephardi Zionism was not, nor did it perceive itself to be anti-religious. Unlike European Zionism, it did not represent the latest stage of a *Kulturkampf* within Jewry. Secondly, Sephardi Jews did not have to worry at first about addressing a Gentile audience that might cast aspersions upon their political loyalty to the state and their cultural loyal to the society the way Jews in Western and Central Europe had to do. Zionism did not threaten Sephardi Jews in the same way — at least not at first. This was to change, however, after the First World War with the rise of nationalism in the Islamic lands.

Most of the early Zionist societies in the Oriental Jewish communities included their spiritual leaders, who were frequently officers of the associations. In Morocco, Tunisia, and Libya in particular, the rabbis perceived Zionism as a thoroughly natural expression of Judaism. As A. Torczyner, an emissary of the World Zionist Organization wrote after a visit to Tunis in 1913:

> Opposition, especially of the sort we find here in Europe is non-existent. The God-fearing regard our movement with warmth and reverence. When I addressed Agudat Zion in Tunis, among the audience were truly religious old people and members of the rabbinical court of justice. The Chief Rabbi, who is sick, apologized for his having withdrawn from the organization. It was the same in Sfax.[15]

Where there was opposition to Zionism among Oriental Jewry, it was from circles within the Alliance Israélite Universelle, which had been overtly tepid and covertly hostile to Zionism since its inception, and from members of the small, wealthy Jewish upper class. Zionism, in the words of a young member of the Alexandrian Jewish elite, was simply "very unchic" in the

[15] Central Zionist Archives (Jerusalem) Z 3/751, letter to Nahum Sokolow (September 26, 1913), quoted in Michel Abitbol, "Zionist Activity in the Maghreb," *The Jerusalem Quarterly* 21 (1981), p. 65. For examples of rabbis actively involved in the Zionist movement, see Stillman, *The Jews of Arab Lands in Modern Times,* pp. 73, 74, 76, 77, 79, 308, and 321.

eyes of most of his set.[16] Genuine religious opposition to the movement remained virtually nonexistent. The only strongly outspoken rabbinical opponent of Jewish nationalism was Sassoon Khadduri, who served as Chief Rabbi of Baghdad from 1927–1929 and was president of the community council from 1932–1949. He originally supported the movement, but then became its implacable foe in the late 1920s. Concerned by the rise of a militant Arab nationalism that had come to totally identify itself with the Arab cause in Palestine, Rabbi Khadduri rejected Zionism solely for political reasons, believing that only in this way was there any hope of protecting Iraqi Jewry from persecution. His pronouncements were never of a theological character. He remained the leading Jewish spokesman against Zionism in the Muslim world until his death in 1971. Even Ḥayyim Nahum, the French-educated, politically active Chief Rabbi of Egypt, who was never a friend of Zionism, studiously avoided the scathing denunciations of the sort made by Khadduri, even when under considerable pressure to do so. The worldly Nahum Effendi, who had been the last Ḥakham Bashi of the Ottoman Empire, and a Turkish diplomat in the immediate post-war years before coming to Egypt, also never used any theological arguments against Zionism. Both Khadduri and Nahum — who were themselves very different from one another — are exceptional figures, untypical of the Eastern Jewish rabbinate in many respects, and certainly neither of them may be

[16] The remark was made by Ralph Harari, one of the few Zionist members of his class. See Gudrun Krämer, *The Jews in Modern Egypt, 1914–1952* (University of Washington Press: Seattle, 1989), p. 194. As to the Alliance's attitudes toward the Jewish national movement — in its publications, it maintained on the whole a studied, but frosty neutrality, but in the private correspondence between Paris headquarters and the Alliance school directors and other representatives in the field, Zionism is referred to with the utmost abuse and invective.

considered in any way representative of the religious community's attitudes toward Zionism.[17]

In fact, Zionism touched deep-seated spiritual chords within Oriental Jewry. These chords were not purely religious in the modern European sense since in the Islamic world, and in Sephardi Judaism generally, confessional community traditionally was understood in a corporate, national sense. The Zionist movement made modest, but not insignificant inroads into most of the major urban Ladino- and Judaeo-Arabic-speaking communities of the Islamic world in the late nineteenth and early twentieth century. It succeeded in arousing considerable popular enthusiasm in the wake of the Balfour Declaration, the Allied victory, and the San Remo Conference. In 1917, for example thousands of Jews gathered in Cairo and Alexandria in support of the Balfour Declaration with all of the communal rabbinical leadership in attendance. Similar mass scenes greeted Chaim Weizmann and the Zionist Commission when they passed through Egypt the following year.[18]

In Tunis, Jews celebrated the Allies' victory by marching through the streets in noisy demonstrations waving the Zionist flag. In a burst of semi-messianic enthusiasm, several hundred Jewish families emigrated from Morocco to Palestine in the immediate post-war years much to the chagrin of the French authorities, the Alliance, and the still small francophile Jewish elite. There was a similar immigration from Iraq at this time, comprising a little over one thousand individuals, with smaller numbers coming from Syria and Libya. Modern Hebrew schools, cultural associations, student and youth groups, and Maccabi

[17] For Khadduri on Zionism, see Stillman, *The Jews of Arab Lands in Modern Times,* pp. 102, 386–389. Concerning Nahum Effendi's ambiguous relationship to Zionism, see Esther Benbassa, *Un grand rabbin sepharade en politique, 1892–1923* (Presses du CNRS: Mesnil-sur-l'Estrée, 1990), pp. 33–48, 60–62, *et passim.* Gudrun Krämer, *The Jews in Modern Egypt, 1914–1952,* pp. 97, 163–164, 192, and 195.

[18] See Stillman, *The Jews of Arab Lands in Modern Times,* pp. 307–308; Krämer, *The Jews in Modern Egypt,* p. 184.

sports clubs — all with a strong Jewish national orientation — sprang up all over North Africa and the Near East.[19]

Widespread sympathy for Zionism among Sephardi and Oriental Jews rarely translated itself into active participation in the Zionist movement. Because of the opposition of nationalist governments, colonial authorities, or popular Muslim hostility, membership in Zionist associations was always extremely limited, except in Tunisia. Even many of those Eastern Jewish communities that did have Zionist associations rarely sent delegates to the early World Zionist Congresses as they were entitled to do. There are a number of reasons for this. First, few Jews in the Muslim world had much if any experience with elected parliamentary representation of any sort. Furthermore, Western and Central Europe, where the congresses were held prior to the First World War, were psychologically as well as physically far away. But most importantly, for many Sephardi and Oriental Jews, especially the more traditional ones, the World Zionist Organization and its leaders were reverentially regarded as being engaged in a divinely ordained enterprise that required only their unquestioning loyalty. As Zvi Yehuda has noted concerning the early Moroccan Zionists (and the same might be said for those in many other Islamic countries at that time), they demonstrated "an unlimited faith in the WZO and its leadership, to the extent that they were completely uninterested in obtaining representation in

---

[19] For Morocco, see the Alliance Israélite Universelle documents and reports translated in Stillman, *The Jews of Arab Lands in Modern Times*, pp. 314–317; and also Doris Bensimon-Donath, *Immigrants d'Afrique du Nord en Israël: évolution et adaptation* (Editions Anthropos: Paris, 1970), p. 64 and the sources cited there in n. 81. For Iraq, see Zvi Yehuda, "Aliya from Iraq in the Early 1920s: Survey and Problematics," in *From Babylon to Jerusalem* (Iraqi Jews Traditional Culture Center, Institute for Research on Iraqi Jewry: Tel Aviv, 1980), pp. 3–16 [in Hebrew]. For Syria, see the documentation from the Sephardi Community Council of Jerusalem in Stillman, ibid., pp. 329–330. For Libya, see the unpublished documents in the Central Zionist Archives (Jerusalem) Z 4/1620. For the growth of schools and clubs, see Stillman, ibid., pp. 81–83.

the WZO's institutions."[20] This political passivity would be abandoned only by a small core of the most modernist and secularist elements of the Sephardi and Oriental Jewish communities during the course of the twentieth century,[21] but it remained the hallmark of the more traditional majority all the way up to the time of their mass exodus and for sometime thereafter in their new homeland. It is significant that, when that traditional majority finally did find its political voice in the Jewish State, one of its principal expressions was decidedly religious in parties such as Tami and now Shas.

There were, of course, a variety of factors of push and pull that impelled the Sephardi and Oriental Jews to depart en masse for the newly-founded State of Israel in the late nineteen forties, fifties, and early sixties. These factors included the political, social, and economic situations prevailing in the countries in which they had been living. But there can be no doubt that their response to these factors was conditioned by their own indigenous form of Zionism. This traditional Sephardi Zionism was deeply rooted in their culture. It had been given frequent expression throughout history from Judah ha-Levi in the twelfth century, to the large-scale resettlement by Iberian exiles in the sixteenth century, and the personal ʿaliyah of thousands of individuals throughout the ages. This Sephardi traditional Zionism underwent an indigenous revival from within during the nineteenth century in no small measure as a genuine religious response to modern times.

---

[20] Zvi Yehuda, "The Place of Aliyah in Moroccan Jewry's Conception of Zionism," *Studies in Zionism* 6:2 (1985), p. 200. This subject is discussed at length in Yehuda's unpublished doctoral dissertation, *Organized Zionism in Morocco: 1900–1948* (Hebrew University: Jerusalem, 1981), vol. 1, pp. 116–120 [in Hebrew].

[21] Already in the 1930s, some Sephardi Zionists began to feel that they were not being represented — or worse, ignored. See Stillman, *The Jews of Arab Lands in Modern Times*, pp. 90–91, 322–323, 329–330, and 340–341.

FOUR

After Modernity: Popular Reassertions, Ashkenazified Religiosity, and other Contemporary Trends

Most of the venerable Sephardi and Oriental Jewish communities that existed until the middle of this century are no more. Some, such as the Sephardi communities of Greece and the neighboring Balkan countries, were nearly exterminated during the Second World War. Most of the others, however, which were situated in the Arab lands, Turkey, Iran, and Central Asia, lost all or most of their inhabitants to mass emigration. Those Jews now live in the State of Israel, where until the recent enormous influx of Russian Jews, they and their descendants comprised a majority of the country's Jewish population. The Sephardi and Oriental Jews are now beginning to put their own distinctive imprint on Israel's evolving society, and at the same time are being influenced and transformed by their new, intimate daily contact with their Ashkenazi coreligionists. A large number of North African Jews have also settled in France, where they too now constitute a majority of the Jews in their adopted home. The Sephardim of France have not merely made an imprint upon French Jewry, but have totally transformed it. (The last two chief rabbis of France were both born in North Africa.) Smaller concentrations of Sephardim have established themselves, in North and South America, and in several European countries, including Spain itself.

The small Sephardi Jewish communities that have stayed behind in their original lands are now no more than vestigial remnants. They are for all intents and purposes moribund.[1] Today, it is primarily in Israel and to a certain extent in France that one can witness the ongoing response (religious and otherwise) of Sephardi and Oriental Jews to modern times.

A great deal has been written about the mass ᶜaliyah and the absorption of these Jews into the Jewish State. Much of the literature deals with the social problems of immigration, absorption, and Israeli policies.[2] The so-called "Ingathering of the Exiles" (*qibbuṣ galuyyot*) by the nascent Jewish State was by any standards a stupendous undertaking. It was also by all accounts a difficult homecoming for many of the new immigrants, particularly for Sephardi and Oriental Jews. Some of them had come fleeing from immediate or potential dangers in their former countries, but almost all of them were swept up in a wave of semi-messianic enthusiasm that emanated from the traditional Sephardi form of Zionism that we have already discussed. Like the new immigrants pouring in from the ruins of Ashkenazi Europe, the Oriental Jews underwent considerable hardship during the early years — the ramshackle transit camps (*maᶜabarot*), food rationing, and hard physical labor. But they experienced other problems that were not shared by their Ashkenazi fellow immigrants.

The Promised Land in which they had arrived had been founded by pioneers from Eastern and Central Europe. Its culture and institutions were already in place and were stamped with a

---

[1] For the most recent survey of most of these communities, excluding the Balkans, see Norman A. Stillman, "Fading Shadows of the Past: Jews in the Islamic World, " in *Survey of Jewish Affairs 1989*, ed. William Frankel (Basil Blackwell Ltd.: Oxford, 1989), pp. 157–170.

[2] One of the early classics in this field is S. N. Eisenstadt, *The Absorption of Immigrants: A Comparative Study Based Mainly on the Jewish Community in Palestine and the State of Israel* (The Free Press: Glencoe, Illinois, 1955), which contains a considerable bibliography. Two other important early studies are Joseph B. Schechtman, *On Wings of Eagles: The Plight, Exodus, and Homecoming of Oriental Jewry* (Thomas Yoseloff: New York and London, 1961); and Doris Bensimon-Donath, *Immigrants d'Afrique du Nord en Israël: évolution et adaptation* (Editions Anthropos: Paris, 1970).

specifically European socialist, utopian character. The regnant form of Zionism and of Jewish culture was that which had evolved in Ashkenazi Europe and represented the radical spectrum of the Haskala. Despite the secularist, indeed antireligious, bent of most members of the dominant elite, there were also religious Jews among the founding fathers and a place for state-sanctioned religion. But the official establishment Judaism was also primarily Ashkenazi. (The Ottoman office of Rishon le-Ṣiyyon continued to exist, but alongside the more influential Ashkenazi Chief Rabbinate that had been created under the Mandate). Thus, for the Sephardi ʿolim there was a particular form of culture shock that awaited them.

The usual traumas of immigration into a new country and society were exacerbated for the Sephardim by other factors, not least of which were the attitudes of the veteran Israelis (*ha-vatiqim*) who related to them on the basis of paternalism and cultural inequality. One widespread sentiment within the secular elite was that the new immigrants from Asia and Africa constituted another "generation of the wilderness" (*dor ha-midbar*). Like the motley crew of slaves that came out of Egypt, they had to die out, so that in the words of the anthropologists Moshe Shokeid and Shlomo Deshen, "the younger generation could be inculcated with the values, beliefs, and practices of the veterans."[3] In other words, in the eyes of the secular Ashkenazi establishment the religious and cultural heritage of the Sephardi and Oriental immigrants was completely devoid of redeeming qualities. ("We do not want a Levantine state," was the oft-repeated shibboleth of the governing elite, including David Ben-Gurion himself.) The Mizraḥi (modern Orthodox) Zionist members of the elite, were more tolerant of the religious heritage of the Sephardi newcomers — but only somewhat more tolerant. They looked favorably only upon those religious traditions and practices that were shared by all observant Jews everywhere, but not upon those that were unique to individual Sephardi and

[3] Moshe Shokeid and Shlomo Deshen, *Distant Relations: Ethnicity and Politics among Arabs and North African Jews in Israel* (Praeger: New York, 1982), p. 4.

Oriental communities, especially those rituals and beliefs that might be described as "folk religion" or "popular religion." They shared the secular veterans' perception that their Eastern brethren came from exotic, but primitive societies, and as such their regional traditions were better abandoned.

On the whole, and in spite of many mistakes that were made, everyone had the best of intentions. The founding fathers felt it their sacred duty to absorb these lost members of the tribe, and the newcomers passionately desired to be part of Israeli society. However, by the very nature of the relationship, misunderstandings, disappointments, and recriminations on both sides were inevitable. The Sephardi-Ashkenazi tensions of the late 1950s, the '60s and the '70s were the direct result of some of the failures of the state's social policies on the one hand, and the bad feelings engendered by the attitudes of the Ashkenazi establishment on the other. This intercommunal tension has also been the subject of a considerable body of sociological literature.[4] Less attention has been devoted to the religious responses of the Sephardi immigrants to their new environment.[5]

[4] Several representative examples of this large corpus of literature with abundant bibliographical references to other works are: Sammy Smooha, *Israel: Pluralism and Conflict* (University of California Press: Berkeley and Los Angeles, 1978); Yochanan Peres, *Ethnic Relations in Israel* 2nd ed. (Sifriat Poʿalim and Tel Aviv University: Tel Aviv, 1977) [in Hebrew]; Eliezer Ben-Rafael, *The Emergence of Ethnicity: Cultural Groups and Social Conflict in Israel* (Greenwood Press: Westport, Conn., and London, 1982).

[5] Among the important exceptions to this general lack of interest in the religious responses of Sephardi and Oriental immigrants to their new environment are the numerous studies of the Israeli anthropologists Shlomo Deshen and Moshe Shokeid who deal with religion in addition to other social phenomena. See, for example, their *The Predicament of Homecoming: Cultural and Social Life of North African Immigrants in Israel* (Cornell University Press: Ithaca and London, 1974); idem, *The Generation of Transition: Continuity and Change Among North African Immigrants in Israel* (Ben Zvi Institute: Jerusalem, 1977) [in Hebrew]; Shlomo Deshen, "Religion Among Middle Eastern Immigrants in Israel," in *Israel — A Developing Society*, ed. Asher Arian (Van Gorcum: Assen, The Netherlands, 1980), pp. 235–246; idem, "The Religion of Middle Eastern Immigrants," *The Jerusalem Quarterly* 13 (Autumn 1979), pp. 98–110; and Moshe Shokied, "Cultural Ethnicity in Israel: The Case of Middle Eastern Jews' Religiosity," in *AJS Review* 9:2 (1984), pp. 247–271.

For some of the newcomers, such as the Jews of Kurdistan, the High Atlas Mountains and the Sahara, or the isolated highlands of Yemen, this was their first real encounter with modernity. But for most, that encounter had already taken place before coming to Israel, albeit in some cases to a greater degree than others. The totality and the abruptness of the change in their world, in their entire frame of reference, constituted for them what might be called with some justification a post-modern condition.[6]

At first, the Sephardi newcomers were so-to-speak "religiously invisible." As with so much else in the early days of Israeli statehood, the new Sephardi immigrants were dependent upon the establishment institutions even in matters of religion. The Ministry of Religious Affairs provided houses of worship, prayer books, and an official, state-salaried rabbinate. The Ministry of Education provided religiously-oriented public schools. And the religious political parties offered various forms of patronage. Some of the traditional spiritual leaders who came to Israel with their communities experienced a loss of their authority. Young Sephardim who entered the religious youth movements or went on to higher religious education usually found themselves in an Ashkenazi environment. Since most of the rabbinical colleges were also European-founded, new Sephardi rabbis were often trained in the Ashkenazi orthodox fashion with its different world outlook, its very distinct approach to piety, and even its own distinctive dress code.

At the same time, there was the powerful antireligious counterforce of the secular Zionist political and cultural elite which dominated the country and was also Ashkenazi. It too provided education, political and economic patronage, and other benefits and blandishments. It contributed also to the weakening of

---

[6] Jean-François Lyotard, *The Postmodern Condition: A Report on Knowledge*, trans. Geoff Bennington and Brian Massumi (University of Minnesota Press: Minneapolis, 1989); David Gross, *The Past in Ruins: Tradition and the Critique of Modernity* (University of Massachusetts Press: Amherst, 1992), pp. 59–61. But see the objections to this notion in Anthony Giddens, *The Consequences of Modernity* (Stanford University Press: Stanford, 1990), pp. 149–150.

traditional authority, not only of old-time spiritual leaders, but of the entire older generation.

Sephardi Jewry in Israel found that the fortunes of its "redemption" had placed it in a subordinate position within a society offering two dominant models of European Jewish responses to modernity — a secular national type and an Ashkenazi religious type. After the initial shock and passivity, it came to respond in turn in a variety of ways.

One response was a decline in religious observance among members of the younger generation. This was something that social scientists (and social planners) had predicted. But the decline did not translate into the kind of wholesale disaffection from religion that characterized much of Ashkenazi secularity. Two decades after the founding of the State, a survey of high school students showed that among the Sephardi pupils surveyed a majority of those who did not define themselves as "religious" (*dati*), chose to identify themselves as "traditional" (*masorati*), and this was nearly half of all Sephardi students. In fact, only about one in five declared themselves to be "non-religious" (*ḥilloni*) as compared to just over half of Ashkenazi students surveyed who defined themselves in that way.[7] "Traditional" in the Israeli context means partial observance of the *miṣvot* (religious commandments). This can range from synagogue attendance only on major holidays and family occasions to regular Sabbath attendance, and from more or less strict maintenance of the dietary laws only at home to their observance on the outside as well (something which is, to be sure, much easier in Israel than in the Diaspora). It was not uncommon to find *masorati* Sephardim who attended Sabbath services on Saturday morning and went to a football match or the beach the same afternoon. These widespread compromises with the general Israeli secular environment were treated — and for the

[7] Simon N. Herman, *Israelis and Jews: The Continuity of an Identity* (Random House: New York, 1970), p. 130, Table 97. The terms *dati, masorati,* and *ḥilloni* are Israeli neologisms which are not based in historical Jewish usage. They are in fact modern categorizations.

most part still are treated — with the traditional tolerance by the Sephardi religious sector. As the lay leader of a small Sephardi congregation in Tel Aviv related to the anthropologist Moshe Shokeid in the late 1970s,

> [H]e was careful not to burden the younger congregants with heavy religious demands. He knew that some of them did not wear a skullcap on weekdays and probably drove cars on the Sabbath, "but what is really important is that they come to the synagogue."[8]

Despite a decline in synagogue attendance among young adults, synagogues maintained their centrality in most Sephardi and Oriental communities. It has remained a point of pride for most neighborhoods to have an ethnic communal synagogue.[9]

One manifestation of Sephardi and Oriental religiosity that has reasserted itself with considerable vitality in the Israeli setting is the very one that the Ashkenazi religious establishment had tried to discourage, namely non universal Jewish rites that were part of local traditions in the Diaspora. These forms of popular religion include the celebration of non-canonical holidays such as the North African Mimouna or the Kurdish Saharani and the widespread veneration of holy men (*saddiqim*), both living and dead, and the celebration of pilgrimages and other special commemorations connected with the death days of these saints (*hillulot*).

---

[8] Shokeid, "Cultural Ethnicity in Israel: The Case of Middle Eastern Jews' Religiosity," p. 257.

[9] Concerning the decline of attendance by young adults in ethnic synagogues, see Shlomo Deshen, "The Ethnic Synagogue: Patterns of Religious Change in Israel, "in *The Integration of Immigrants from Different Countries of Origin in Israel*, ed. S. N. Eisenstadt and A. Zloczower (Magnes Press: Jerusalem, 1969), pp. 66–73 [in Hebrew]. On the synagogue's continued centrality, see Ben-Rafael, *The Emergence of Ethnicity*, p. 93; and cf. also the mixed data in Shokeid, "Cultural Ethnicity in Israel: The Case of Middle Eastern Jews' Religiosity," pp. 256–259, which I interpret to be supportive of Ben-Rafael's generalization. Most recently, Ben-Rafael and Sharot have offered plausible explanations why Sephardi and Oriental Jews born or raised in Israel are more likely to continue attending ethnic synagogues, whereas their Ashkenazi counterparts are more likely to attend interethnic ones. See Eliezer Ben-Rafael and Stephen Sharot, *Ethnicity, Religion and Class in Israeli Society* (Cambridge University Press: Cambridge and New York, 1991), pp. 75–77.

Both the festivities of these holidays and the pilgrimages attract enormous numbers of people, young and old, of all levels of religiosity, education, and socioeconomic status. They represent an act of what David Gross has called "reappropriating tradition through its traces."[10]

The Mimouna and the Sahrani are as much statements of ethnic pride and identity as they are religious manifestations, somewhat parallel to Saint Patrick's Day in the United States.[11] The required appearance of Israeli politicians of all stripes to "press the flesh" at these celebrations, as well as the participation of assorted non-ethnic merrymakers, who become honorary ethnics for the day, are indicative of the general perception that these are ethnic, not religious occasions. But this superficial overview masks a genuine spiritual aspect for many of the celebrants. I have personally participated in numerous Mimouna celebrations since I am married into a Moroccan family and have many Moroccan friends. The traditional Mimouna observances complete with blessings and ritual foods are reserved for private homes on the evening Passover ends as an *isru ḥag,* a sort of minor holiday that occurs at the conclusion of each of the three major festivals. Many Moroccans look askance at the wild crowds that fill the nation's parks the next day for barbecues, belly dancing, and political speeches. However, even the public Mimouna celebrations are viewed by their organizers as more than just a day for what in the American context would be called "putting on the green." This became apparent to me during a year I spent in Jerusalem when together with my colleague/wife,

---

[10] David Gross, *The Past in Ruins: Tradition and the Critique of Modernity* (University of Massachusetts Press: Amherst, 1992), pp. 92–106.

[11] Concerning the history and practices associated with the Mimouna, see Harvey E. Goldberg, "The Mimuna and the Minority Status of Moroccan Jews," *Ethnology* 17:1 (1978), pp. 75–87.; Norman A. Stillman, "Moslems and Jews: The Connections Between the Mimouna Festival and Moslem Jewish Coexistence," *Jerusalem Post Supplement* (April 3, 1983), p. 6. On the Saharani, see J. Halper and H. Abramovitz, "The Saharanei Celebration in Kurdistan and Israel," in *Jews of the Middle East: Anthropological Perspectives Past and Present*, eds. Shlomo Deshen and Moshe Shokeid (Schocken Books: Tel Aviv, 1984), [in Hebrew].

I was appointed to a committee for planning the national Mimouna program. A distinguished Moroccan-born Israeli scholar, who also happened to be religious (on the modern end of the spectrum — i.e., "knitted kippa"), explained to the other members of the committee what he hoped we could accomplish. He said that he did not want to preserve a separate Moroccan form of Judaism for his sons. They should be part of a developing Israeli Judaism. He wanted, however, to bequeath something from the Moroccan heritage to his sons and all Israelis, and that was the Mimouna. He envisaged it as a modern-day parallel to Persian Jewry giving Purim to all Jews during the Second Temple period. His goal was brought one step further that same year when the Rishon le-Ṣiyyon, the Sephardi Chief Rabbi of Israel, gave his formal public blessing to the Mimouna observance.

The other vigorous reassertion of Sephardi and Oriental religiosity that has grown tremendously over the past three decades is hagiolatry. The veneration of holy men and the performance of pilgrimages organized around their grave sites was an important part of popular piety in many parts of the Sephardi world, and most particularly in North Africa. Even in the diaspora there were many Sephardi rabbinical authorities who disapproved of some of the aspects of this saint worship, just as Ashkenazi Misnagdim condemned the hagiolatry of the Hasidim. The Sephardi rabbis, however, despite their objections, generally made accommodations for these practices because they were so ubiquitous, in order to keep them within halakhic bounds.[12]

During the first decade following the mass ʿaliyah, there was little public manifestation of saint veneration. This was due in part to the initial shock and passivity of the Sephardi immigrants as they adjusted to their new surroundings. It was also probably due to the hard times and still primitive conditions prevailing in

[12] There is an enormous literature on Jewish hagiolatry in the Maghreb. See Issachar Ben-Ami, *Saint Veneration Among the Jews in Morocco* (Magnes Press: Jerusalem, 1984) [in Hebrew], where there is an extensive bibliography.

the young state which made large scale pilgrimages to distant parts of the country unfeasible. The observance of saints' days, or *hillulot* (an Aramaic word meaning "a wedding celebration") with their commemorative collations, chanting of liturgical poetry, and recitation of mystical texts such as the Zohar, was confined primarily to the home. In the 1960s, synagogues named after holy men began to proliferate, and some became sites of major annual *hillulot* (as for example, the synagogue of Rabbi Dawid u-Mushe in Safed). It was also at this time that pilgrimages to the graves of holy men buried in Israel began to attract more and more people. These pilgrimages, which had been designated *ziyara* (Arabic for "visit") in the diaspora, came to be called *ʿaliyah le-regel,* the evocative biblical phrase meaning "going up on foot" that was used for the three annual festival pilgrimages of ancient Temple times. The great *hillula* par excellence on Lag B'Omer at the grave of Rabbi Simeon Bar Yoḥai at Meron in the Galilee became the single most important pilgrimage attracting over 100,000 people (a prodigious crowd by Israeli standards). Although North Africans constitute the majority of pilgrims at Meron, there are also large numbers of other Sephardim, as well as a considerable minority of Ashkenazi Hasidim, who come to give their three-year-old sons their ritual first haircut. Many young Sephardim, including those who are less formally observant continue to attend the *hillula*. The anthropologist Moshe Shokeid suggests that they are "[d]rawn, among other things, by the entertainment and social activities" which the *hillulot* provide. But I would add that there is a strong sense of traditional *communitas* in the Turnerian sense, which has always been at the very heart of the religious experience at such gatherings.[13]

[13] Shokeid, "Cultural Ethnicity in Israel: The Case of Middle Eastern Jews' Religiosity," p. 262. For the notion of *communitas* as one of the primary features of any pilgrimage, see Victor Turner, "Pilgrimage as Social Process," in his *Dramas, Fields, and Metaphors: Symbolic Action in Human Society* (Cornell University Press: Ithaca, New York, 1974), pp. 167–230. For early observations on the Meron pilgrimage and other *hillulot*, see Shokeid and Deshen, *The Generation of Transition: Continuity and Change Among North African Immigrants in Israel*, pp. 93–121.

One very interesting phenomenon is the spontaneous emergence of new pilgrimage sites in Israel and the addition of newly recognized individuals to the pantheon of *ṣaddiqim*. Among the more notable are the *hillulot* around the graves of the Tunisian Rabbi Ḥayyim Ḥuri, who died in Beer Sheba in 1957, and of the Moroccan thaumaturge, Rabbi Israel Abu Ḥaṣera, known as the Baba Sali, who died in the Negev town of Netivot in 1984 and whose portrait now adorns the walls of countless kiosks and (Middle Eastern style) restaurants throughout Israel. Both of these pilgrimages now attract ten of thousands of participants of all ages as well as a steady stream of devotees throughout the year. The proliferation of saints' shrines in Israeli development towns, (which in fact are often the most under-developed communities in the country) may be seen in part as a subconscious religious response to the physical, economic, and social isolation of many of these places and at the same time as the means of establishing a deep spiritual intimacy with the new surroundings.[14]

The vigorous reemergence of saint veneration may also be viewed as a psychological response to the strains of military service and frequent wars. The Israeli folklorist Issachar Ben-Ami has observed an increase in reported miracles by the saints during military conflicts. The dates for a number of *hillulot* for local *ṣaddiqim* were fixed on the days a war ended, or in the case of Ḥoni ha-Meᶜaggel, the miracle worker of the Second Temple Period buried in Hatzor, on Israeli Independence Day.[15]

---

[14] Alex Weingrod, *The Saint of Beersheba* (State University of New York Press: Albany, 1990); E. Ben-Ari and Y. Bilu, "Saints' Sanctuaries in Israeli Development Towns: On a Mechanism of Urban Transformation," *Urban Anthropology* 16:2 (1987), pp. 243–272. The shrine built around Baba Sali's grave has become a popular place for Bar Mitzvah celebrations, and approximately fifty families a week pay the considerable sum of NIS 1000 (over $300) to take out and read a Torah scroll. See Tom Sawicki, "Inside the World of Mystic Healers," *The Jerusalem Report* (January 27, 1994), p. 14.

[15] Issacher Ben-Ami, "Le-Ḥeqer Folklor ha-Milḥama: Motiv ha-Qedoshim," in *Sefer Dov Sadan*, eds. S. Werses, N. Rotenstreich, and C. Shmeruk (Ha-Kibbutz Ha-Me'uḥad: Jerusalem, 1977), pp. 87–104.

Shlomo Deshen, always a sensitive and perceptive student of the sociology of religion, offers another explanation for the exponential growth of saint veneration and pilgrimages. This reinvigorated hagiolatry, he argues, emerges from a decline of traditional religious observance, on the one hand, coupled with continued adherence to fundamental beliefs (such as the existence of God, Divine Providence, reward and punishment, the messianic redemption, the chosenness of the Jewish people, the status of the sages, and the sanctity of the Land of Israel), on the other. Pilgrimage and veneration of *ṣaddiqim* offer religious practice that is easy to perform and yet highly efficacious if one has faith and truly believes.[16] In other words, this is a spiritual response to what is an essentially a modern existential situation of Jews who have chosen not to live in accordance with all of the demands of traditional halakhic Judaism.

There is yet another Sephardi religious response to the challenges of modern life in Israel, and this response comes from within the religious part of community itself, which is still a significant sector. (The survey of high school students that was cited earlier showed that over one third of Sephardi pupils identified themselves as "religious" (*dati*), as compared to just over a fifth of their Ashkenazi peers.)[17] I would call this response Ashkenazification; that is, the adoption of some of the modes and norms, and — no less significant — the *mentalités* of Ashkenazi religiosity.

Over the past four decades, most Sephardi religious youth in Israel have attended the ordinary public religious schools (*bate*

[16] Shlomo Deshen, "La religiosité des Orientaux en Israël," in *Recherches sur la culture des Juifs d'Afrique du Nord*, ed. Issachar Ben-Ami (Communauté Israélite Nord-Africaine: Jerusalem, 1991), p. 362. For other thoughts on the impetus behind the growth of saint veneration in Israel, see also the important essay of Yoram Bilu, "Personal Motivation and Social Meaning in the Revival of Hagiolatric Traditions among Moroccan Jews in Israel," in *Tradition, Innovation, Conflict: Jewishness and Judaism in Contemporary Israel,* eds. Zvi Sobel and Benjamin Beit-Hallahmi (State University of New York Press: Albany, 1991), pp. 47–69.

[17] See n. 6 above.

sefer mamlakhtiyyim datiyyim), but a few went to advanced talmudical colleges. Since there were until recently relatively few Sephardi rabbinical schools of this sort, most of these young Sephardi rabbinical students studied in academies which had been founded under Ashkenazi auspices. Some Sephardi students even gained entry into the elite Lithuanian yeshivot of Ponevezh and Slobodka in Bnei Berak. These institutions, whether of the neo-Orthodox "knitted kippa" or the ultra-Orthodox "black hat" variety, taught according to the Ashkenazi yeshiva curriculum which differed significantly in both content and style from the traditional Sephardi yeshiva education. In the former, the curriculum consisted almost entirely of the Talmud and the later commentaries and supercommentaries studied through the discipline of theoretical casuistry, and the emphasis was placed almost exclusively upon the authority of texts. Whereas in the latter, the traditional education had been more broadly based, including such subjects as Bible and Hebrew prosody to the core of talmudic studies. In addition to textual authority, the Sephardi yeshiva also placed considerable store in living tradition, and the emphasis of its program was on the practical application of halakha needed for communal service.

The young Sephardi rabbis who came out of the Ashkenazi institutions were assimilated into the Eastern European yeshiva subculture. Some went so far as to learn Yiddish and to adopt the Ashkenazi *nosaḥ*, or rite, for their personal prayer. Those that emerged from the *ḥaredi* yeshivot dressed in the distinguishing black attire of the ultra-Orthodox. The new small Sephardi yeshivas that they founded, as the Sephardi scholar and intellectual Daniel Elazar ruefully observes, imitate Ashkenazi models "in ways that inevitably cause them to be inferior."[18] It was out of this milieu that there emerged organizations like *Rabbi Reuben Elbaz's* Or ha-Ḥayyim ("The Light of Life") *baʿal teshuva* movement to bring young penitents back into the fold of

---

[18] Daniel J. Elazar, *The Other Jews: The Sephardim Today* (Basic Books: New York, 1989), p. 201.

strict religious observance. Elbaz's religious outreach, which is modelled on many similar Ashkenazi ones, has enjoyed considerable success, and by the late 1980s, it boasted having more than 150 schools and clubs throughout Israel.[19]

It was also out of this Ashkenazi yeshiva milieu that the *ḥaredi* political party, Shas (The Sephardi Torah Guardians), was founded in 1983, and now has six seats in the Knesset. The founders were deeply dissatisfied with the blatant discrimination they faced in the Ashkenazi yeshiva circles with regard to status and power, jobs, marital matches, and funding. One of their goals was to form a separate Sephardi *ḥaredi* community with its own schools and communal institutions. The Shas rabbis also aim at creating the same kind of devoted following that the great Ashkenazi ultra-orthodox leaders, such as the Lithuanian yeshiva heads and the Hasidic rebbes, have. The Shas Party looks to Rabbi Ovadia Yosef as its spiritual leader in much the same was as the Yahadut ha-Torah ha-Me'uḥedet (United Torah Judaism) Party looks to Rabbi Eliezer Shach. Actually, Rabbi Shach had been the mentor of many of the Shas founders and had encouraged the formation of the party as a counterpoint to his Hasidic adversaries in the Agudat Yisrael Party. However, the long-simmering alienation of the Shas leaders, including Rabbi Ovadia Yosef, came to a boil during the 1992 election when Rabbi Shach declared in an address before 200 Sephardi rabbis that "Oriental Jews were not yet qualified to lead Israel and the ḥaredi community."[20]

[19] See Pinhas Landau, "The Sephardi Revolution, " *The Jerusalem Post International Edition* (June 27, 1987), p. 11. Shlomo Deshen, "La religiosité deṣ Orientaux en Israël," p. 363, argues that "the phenomenon of returning in penitence does indeed exist here and there among Oriental youth, but it is apparently completely marginal from the quantitative point of view." However, that is debatable.

[20] Sammy Smooha and Don Peretz, "Israel's 1992 Knesset Elections: Are They Critical?," *Middle East Journal* 47:3 (Summer 1993), pp. 453–454. See also Landau, "The Sephardi Revolution," p. 11; and Deshen, "La religiosité des Orientaux en Israël," pp. 359–364.

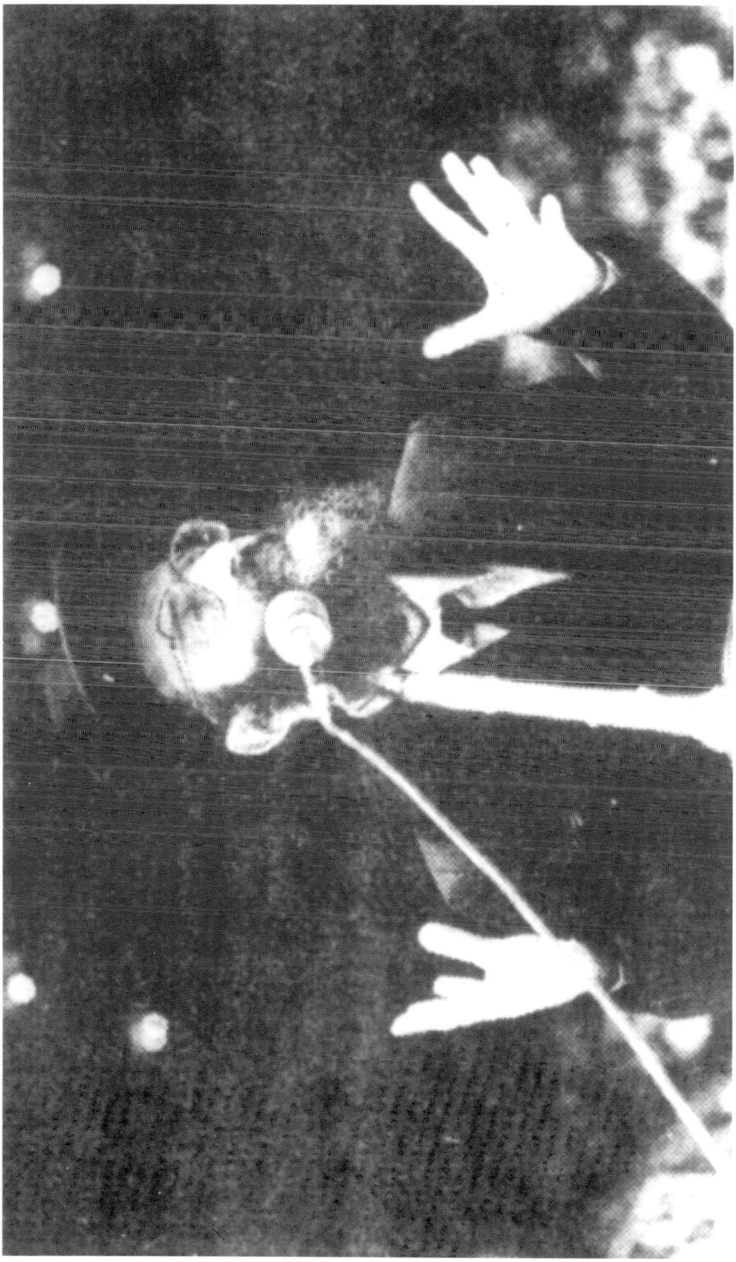

Plate 7 Rabbi Reuben Elbaz of the Or ha-Ḥayyim religious outreach movement preaching to the young. He is dressed in the Ashkenazi "black hat" style.

Plate 8 Rabbi Ovadia Yosef addressing a Shas Party rally in Israel. He is wearing the traditional Ottoman-style robes of the Rishon le-Zion, while the Sephardi rabbis flanking him are dressed in East-European Ashkenazi attire.

Plate 9 Rabbi Ovadia Yosef, former Chief Sephardi Rabbi of Israel in a moment of meditation before addressing a rally in a Tel Aviv sports arena. (Joel Fishman)

Plate 10 Scene from the hillula of Rabbi David u-Moshe at his shrine in Safed, Israel, 1982. *Courtesy of Professor Yoram Bilu.*

Plate 11 Women placing oil and water on the memorial to Rabbi David u-Moshe at his hillula in Safed, Israel, 1982. *Courtesy of Professor Yoram Bilu.*

A great cultural and spiritual gulf divides this new Ashkenazified Sephardi religious elite from the Sephardi masses that they have been courting at the ballot box. Some of the Sephardi ultra-orthodox are contemptuous of traditional Sephardi religiosity. The degree of this contempt is exemplified by a scene witnessed by the anthropologist Deshen when a young Moroccan rabbinical student studying at one of the prestigious Askhenazi yeshivas in Israel got into an altercation with members in his family's synagogue while giving a public lesson on one of his rare visits home. In response to those who disagreed with the interpretations he was giving, he replied that even the least among the students in his yeshiva knew better how to study (religious texts) than the greatest of the rabbis in Morocco![21]

Part of the success of Shas has been the result of protest votes against the Ashkenazi-dominated parties, and part is due to the great veneration with which many traditionalist Sephardim treat their rabbis (even if they have been Ashkenazified).

There has also been some Ashkenazification among the Sephardi masses. The inspiration for this was not from the Lithuanian Misnagdim, but from their Hasidic opponents. For more than four decades the Lubavitcher Ḥabad movement has actively proselytized among Sephardim in North Africa, in France, and in Israel. The Lubavitchers reached far greater numbers of Sephardim by their friendly and non-contemptuous manner and by making accommodations to Sephardi ritual and custom, which in any case has certain important elements in common with Hasidic practice, such as hagiolatry and Lurianic kabbalism. (I was struck when I first began to work in Morocco more than twenty years ago that there were three pictures hanging on the wall of almost every Jewish home I entered — King Ḥassan II, Jacob Abuḥaṣera, a popular Moroccan saint of the nineteenth century, and the Lubavitcher Rebbe.) Another

[21] Deshen, "La religiosité des Orientaux en Israël," p. 360.

reason for the success of the Ḥabad emissaries is that they did — and continue to do — much of their work on a popular level. Furthermore, the Lubavitchers, in contradistinction to the Misnagdim, welcomed into their highest echelons those Sephardim who went to their yeshivas and joined their ranks. Despite their accommodating style, the Lubavitchers grafted their own very specific brand of religiosity onto their Sephardi protégés, and those that actually join the Ḥabad movement are required to take on its special customs and practices.[22]

Whether acculturated by the yeshiva world of the Lithuanian Misnagdim or the proselytizing enthusiasm of the Lubavitcher Hasidim, the Sephardim whom they have touched both in Israel (which I have focussed upon in this chapter) and in France (which I have only mentioned in passing)[23] have assimilated one trait shared by both Ashkenazi groups — a degree of zealousness and an uncompromising spirit that is not only anti-secularist, but anti-every other form of religiosity that does not conform to its standards, that is closed to general culture, and that refuses to look outside the proverbial "four cubits of the law," and even those four cubits are understood in only the most restrictive fashion. This outlook is a far cry from that of traditional Sephardi Judaism. It is a far cry from the spirit of tolerance and openness that has been the hallmark of Sephardi piety. And it is a far cry from the boldness and creativity of Sephardi religious authorities applying the halakha to the challenges of the contemporary world. The Ashkenazified Sephardi trends are

---

[22] Concerning the Lubavitcher network of schools in Morocco, see Michael M. Laskier, *The Alliance Israélite Universelle and the Jewish Communities of Morocco, 1862–1962* (State University of New York Press: Albany, 1983), pp. 248–251. See also Elazar, *The Other Jews: The Sepharadim Today*, p. 111; Deshen, "la religiosité des Orientaux en Israël," p. 361.

[23] For the militancy of contemporary Sephardi religious leaders in France, see the issue of *L'Evenement du Jeudi* devoted to French Jewry, particularly the articles, Claude Askolovitch, "Comment le Judaïsme français s'est laissé grignoter par les intégristes," *L'Evenement du Jeudi*, No. 285 (19–25 avril 1990), pp. 56–61; and Martine Gozlan, "Le truc Sitruk," *ibid*, pp. 62–63.

post-modern responses that seek, like so many so-called fundamentalist religious movements in the late twentieth-century world of today, to escape modernity by returning to the idealized past.[24]

Most Sephardim have not been Ashkenazified. Many communities retain a traditional piety that is without tension. A growing number of younger people are becoming less observant altogether. The present-day Sephardi religious leadership, on the other hand, is not in the traditional mold, and its responses to the challenges of the age appear to be very radically different from those of their predecessors of the last century and a half.

---

[24] See José Faur, "The Shift Towards Extremism," *Jerusalem Post International Edition* (May 14, 1988), p. 8. These responses have also been referred to as "demodernization" or "demodernizing consciousness." See Peter L. Berger, Brigitte Berger, and Hansfried Kellner, *The Homeless Mind: Modernization and Consciousness* (Random House: New York, 1973), pp. 201–230.

BIBLIOGRAPHY

Aben Ṣur, Rabbi Jacob.

Mishpaṭ u-Ṣdaqa be-Yaʿaqov. Alexandria: Farag Ḥayyim Mizraḥi 1894.

Abitbol, Michel.

"Research on Zionism and Aliya of Oriental Jewry — Methodological Aspects," *Peʿamim* 39 (1989) [Hebrew].

"Zionist Activity in the Maghreb," *The Jerusalem Quarterly* 21 (1981).

Agasi, Simeon.

Imre Shimʿon. Jerusalem 1967/68.

Ahavat ha-Qadmonim: Jerusalem: Samuel ha-Levi Zuckerman, 1909.

Alkalai, Judah.

Kitve ha-Rav Yehuda Alkalaʿi. Vol. 1. Edited by Isaac Werfel. Jerusalem: Mosad ha-Rav Kook, 1944.

Angel, Marc D.

Voices in Exile: A Study in Sephardic Intellectual History. Hoboken, New Jersey: Ktav Publishing House, 1991.

Askolovitch, Claude.

"Comment le Judaïsme français s'est laissé grignoter par les intégristes," *L'Evenement du Jeudi,* No. 285 (19–25 avril 1990).

Bashan, Eliezer.

"ʿAl Yaḥasam shel Hakhme Maroqo ba-Me'ot ha-XVIII-XIX le-Ḥovat ha-ʿAliya le-Ereṣ Yisra'el," in *Yehude Ṣefon Afriqa ve-Ereṣ Yisra'el.* Edited by Shalom Bar Asher and Aharon Maman. Jerusalem: Beyaḥad, 1981.

Ben-Ami, Issachar.

Saint Veneration Among the Jews in Morocco. Jerusalem: Magnes Press, 1984 [Hebrew].

"Le-Ḥeqer Folklor ha-Milḥama: Motiv ha-Qedoshim," in *Sefer Dov Sadan.* Edited by S. Verssess, N. Rotenstreich, and C. Shmeruk. Jerusalem: Ha-Kibbutz Ha-Me'uḥad, 1977.

Ben-Ari, E. and Y. Bilu.

"Saints' Sanctuaries in Israeli Development Towns: On a Mechanism of Urban Transformation," *Urban Anthropology* 16 (1987).

Ben-Rafael, Eliezer.

The Emergence of Ethnicity: Cultural Groups and Social Conflict in Israel. Westport, Conn., and London: Greenwood Press, 1982.

and Stephen Sharot. *Ethnicity, Religion and Class in Israeli Society.* Cambridge: Cambridge University Press, 1991.

Ben Simeon, Raphael Aaron.

Umi-Ṣur Devash. Jerusalem: Samuel ha-Levi Zuckerman, 1911/12.

Tuv Miṣrayim. Jerusalem: Defus ha-Rav Samuel ha-Levi Zuckerman, 1908.

Nehar Miṣrayim. Alexandria: Farag Ḥayyim Mizraḥi, 1907/08.

Benbassa, Esther.

Un grand rabbin sepharade en politique, 1892–1923. Mesnil-sur-l'Estrée: Presses du CNRS, 1990.

Bengualíd, Issac.
Va-Yomer Yisḥaq. Jerusalem: Mosdot Va-Yomer Yiṣḥaq, 1977/78.
Bensimon-Donath, Doris.
Immigrants d'Afrique du Nord en Israël: évolution et adaptation. Paris: Editions Anthropos, 1970.
Berger, Peter L.
Pyramids of Sacrifice. New York: Basic Books, 1976.
Berger, Peter L., Brigitte Berger, and Hansfried Kellner.
The Homeless Mind: Modernization and Consciousness. New York: Random House, 1973.
Bilu, Yoram.
"Personal Motivation and Social Meaning in the Revival of Hagiolatric Traditions among Moroccan Jews in Israel," in *Tradition, Innovation, Conflict: Jewishness and Judaism in Contemporary Israel.* Edited by Zvi Sobel and Benjamin Beit-Hallahmi. Albany: State University of New York Press, 1991.
Braslavsky, J.
"Jewish Settlement in Tiberias from Don Joseph Nasi to Ibn Yaish," *Zion* 5 (1940) [Hebrew].
Breuer, Mordechai.
Modernity within Tradition: The Social History of Orthodox Jewry in Imperial Germany. Translated by Elizabeth Petuchowski. New York: Columbia University Press, 1992.
Brunot, Louis and Elie Malka.
Textes judéo-arabes de Fès. Rabat: Typo-Litho Ecole du Livre, 1939.
Chetrit, Joseph.
"New Consciousness of Anomaly and Language: The Beginnings of a Movement of Hebrew Enlightenment in Morocco at the End of the Nineteenth Century," *Miqqedem Umiyyam.* Vol. 2. Edited by Joseph Chetrit and Zvi Yehuda. Haifa: University of Haifa Faculty of the Humanities, 1986 [Hebrew].
"Hebrew National Modernity against French Modernity: The Hebrew Haskalah in North Africa at the End of the Nineteenth Century," *Miqqedem Umiyyam.* Vol. 3. Edited by Joseph Chetrit. Haifa: University of Haifa Faculty of the Humanities, 1990 [Hebrew].
Cohen, Hayyim J.
The Jews of the Middle East, 1860–1972. New York and Toronto: John Wiley & Sons, 1973.
Deshen, Shlomo.
"Baghdad Jewry in Late Ottoman Times: The Emergence of Social Classes and of Secularization," *AJS Review* 19 (1994).
"The Ethnic Synagogue: Patterns of Religious Change in Israel," in *The Integration of Immigrants from Different Countries of Origin in Israel.* Edited by S. N. Eisenstadt and A. Zloczower. Jerusalem: Magnes Press, 1969 [Hebrew].
"La religiosité des Orientaux en Israël." in *Recherches sur la culture des Juifs d'Afrique du Nord.* Edited by Issachar Ben-Ami. Jerusalem: Communauté Israélite Nord-Africaine, 1991.
"Religion Among Middle Eastern Immigrants in Israel," in *Israel — A Developing Society.* Edited by Asher Arian. Assen, The Netherlands: Van Gorcum, 1980.

"The Religion of Middle Eastern Immigrants." *The Jerusalem Quarterly* 13 (Autumn 1979).
Dubnov, Simon M.
History of the Jews in Russian and Poland from the Earliest Times until the Present Day. Vol. 1. Translated by I. Friedlaender. Philadelphia: Jewish Publication Society, 1916–1920.
Dwek, Jacob Saul.
Derekh Emuna. Aleppo: 1913/14.
Eisenstadt, S. N.
The Absorption of Immigrants: A Comparative Study Based Mainly on the Jewish Community in Palestine and the State of Israel. Glencoe, Illinois: The Free Press, 1955.
Tradition, Change, and Modernity. Malabar, Florida: Robert E. Krieger Publishing, 1983.
Elazar, Daniel J.
The Other Jews: The Sephardim Today. New York. Basic Books, 1989.
Elon, Menahem.
"Yiḥudah shel Halakha be-Yahadut Ṣefon Afriqa mi le'aḥar Gerush Sefarad ve-'ad Yamenu," in *Halakha u Fetiḥut Ḥakhme Moroqo ke-Fosqim le-Dorenu*. Edited by Moshe Bar-Yuda. Tel Aviv: ha-Merkaz le-Tarbut ule-Ḥinnukh shel ha-Histadrut, 1985.
Encyclopaedia Judaica. 16 vols. Jerusalem, 1971.
Fargeon, Maurice.
Les Juifs en Egypte depuis les origines jusqu'à ce jour: histoire générale suivie d'un aperçu documentaire. Cairo: Imprimerie Paul Barbey, 1938.
Farḥi, Menahem.
Rav Pe'alim. Constantinople: Defus Avraham Shalto, 1880.
Faur, José.
"Early Zionist Ideals Among Sephardim in the Nineteenth Century," *Judaism* 25 (1976).
Ha-Rav Yisra'el Moshe Hazzan: ha-Ish u-Mishnato. Haifa: Raphael Arbel Academic Publishers, 1978.
"The Shift Towards Extremism," *Jerusalem Post International Edition* (May 14, 1988).
Freimann, Haim.
Seder Qiddushin u-Nesu'in Aḥare Ḥatimat ha-Talmud. Jerusalem: Mossad Ha-Rav Kook, 1964.
Friedman, Menachem.
"Ḥaredim Confront the Modern City," *Studies in Contemporary Jewry*. II. Edited by Peter Y. Medding. Bloomington: Indiana University Press, 1986.
Frumkin, Arieh Leib.
Toledot Ḥakhme Yerushalayim Mi-Shnat H"A R"N la-Yeṣira 'ad H"A TR"L la-Yeṣira. Jerusalem: Defus Solomon, 1928–1930.
Giddens, Anthony.
The Consequences of Modernity. Stanford, California: Stanford University Press, 1990.
Goitein, S. D.
"The Biography of Rabbi Judah ha-Levi in the Light of the Cairo Geniza

Documents," *Proceedings of the American Academy for Jewish Research* 28 (1959).
Goldberg, Harvey.
"Religious Responses Among North African Jews in the Nineteenth and Twentieth Centuries," in *The Uses of Tradition: Jewish Continuity in the Modern Era*. Edited by Jack Wertheimer. New York and Jerusalem: Jewish Theological Seminary of America, 1992.
"The Mimuna and the Minority Status of Moroccan Jews," *Ethnology* 17 (1978).
Green, Arthur.
Tormented Master: A Life of Rabbi Nahman of Bratslav. New York: Schocken, 1981.
Gross, David.
The Past in Ruins: Tradition and the Critique of Modernity. Amherst: University of Massachusetts Press, 1992.
ha-Kohen, Aaron Mendel.
Yad Re"em. Edited by Ḥayyim Naphtali Weisblum. Tel Aviv: 1959/60.
ha-Kohen, Mordekhai.
Higgid Mordecai: Histoire de la Libye et de ses Juifs, lieux d'habitation et coutumes. Edited by Harvey E. Goldberg. Jerusalem: Institut Ben-Zvi, 1978.
ha-Levi, Judah.
The Kuzari: An Argument for the Faith of Israel. Translated by Hartwig Hirschfeld. London: George Routledge & Sons, 1905.
Selected Poems of Jehudah Halevi. Edited by Heinrich Brody and translated by Nina Salaman. Philadelphia: Jewish Publication Society, 1924.
Halper, J. and H. Abramovitz.
"The Saharanei Celebration in Kurdistan and Israel," in *Jews of the Middle East: Anthropological Perspectives Past and Present*. Edited by Shlomo Deshen and Moshe Shokeid. Tel Aviv: Schocken Books, 1984 [Hebrew].
Harel, Yaron.
"A Spiritual Agitation in the East — The Founding of a Reform Community in Aleppo in 1862," *Hebrew Union College Annual* 63 (1992) [Hebrew].
Ḥayyim, Joseph.
Ben Ish Ḥayy. Part 2. Jerusalem: Baqqal, 1977.
Hazan, Ephraim.
"Language and Style in the Poetry of Rabbi David Kayyam," *Pe'amim* 17 (1983) [Hebrew].
Ḥazzan, Elijah.
Zikhron Yerushalayim. Livorno: Elijah Benamozegh, 1874.
Ta'alumot Lev. 6 vols; Vol. 1, Livorno: Elijah Benamozegh, 1879; Vol. 4, Alexandria: Farag Ḥayyim Mizraḥi, 1907.
Neve Shalom. Alexandria: Farag Ḥayyim Mizraḥi, 1893/4.
Ḥazzan, Israel Moses.
She'erit ha-Naḥala: Viku'aḥ. Sho'el u-Meshiv. Alexandria: Tipografia Ottolenghi, 1862.
Words of Peace and Truth. London: Samuel Meldola, 1845.
Herman, Simon N.
Israelis and Jews: The Continuity of an Identity New York: Random House, 1970.

Hertzberg, Arthur.
The Zionist Idea. New York: Atheneum, 1976.
Hirschberg, H. Z. [J. W.].
"The Oriental Jewish Communities," in *Religion in the Middle East: Three Religions in Concord and Conflict*. Vol. 1. Edited by A. J. Arberry. Cambridge: Cambridge University Press, 1969.
Jacobs, Louis.
"The Responsa of Rabbi Joseph Hayyim of Baghdad," in *Perspectives on Jews and Judaism: Essays in Honor of Wolfe Kelman*. Edited by Arthur A. Chiel. New York. The Rabbinical Assembly, 1978.
Kahalon, Yehuda.
"ha Maʿavaq ʿal Demutah ha-Ruḥanit shel ha-ʿEda ha-Yehudit be-Luv ba-Me'a ha-19 uva-ʿAsor ha-Rishon shel ha Me'a ha-ʿEsrim," in *Zakhor Le-Abraham: Mélanges Abraham Elmaleh à l'occasion du cinquième anniversaire de sa mort (21 Adar II 5727)*. Edited by H. Z. Hirschberg. Jerusalem: Comité de la Communauté Marocaine, 1972.
Katz, Jacob.
"Towards a Biography of the Hatam Sofer," in *From East and West: Jews in a Changing Europe, 1750–1870*. Edited by Frances Malino and David Sorkin. Oxford and Cambridge, Mass.: Basil Blackwell, 1990
Out of the Ghetto: The Social Background of Jewish Emancipation, 1770–1870. Cambridge, Mass.: Harvard University Press, 1973.
Tradition and Crisis: Jewish Society at the End ofthe Middle Ages. 2nd ed. Translated by Bernard Dov Cooperman. New York: New York University Press, 1993.
"Meshiḥiyyut u-Le'umiyyut be-Mishnato shel ha-Rav Yehuda Alqalaʿi," in *Shivat Ṣiyyon: Me'assef le-Ḥeqer ha-Ṣiyyonut u-Tqumat Yisra'el*. Vol 4. Edited by B. Dinur and Y. Heilprin. Jerusalem: Ha-Sifriyya ha-Ṣiyyonit, 1956.
Krämer, Gudrun.
The Jews in Modern Egypt, 1914–1952. Seattle: University of Washington Press, 1989.
Kressel, Getzel.
"Protestrabbiner," *Encyclopaedia Judaica*. Vol. 13.
Landau, Jacob.
Jews in Nineteenth-Century Egypt. New York and London: New York University Press and University of London Press, 1969.
Landau, Pinhas.
"The Sephardi Revolution," *The Jerusalem Post International Edition* (June 27, 1987).
Laquer, Walter.
A History of Zionism. New York: Holt, Rinehart and Winston, 1972.
Laskier, Michael M.
The Alliance Israélite Universelle and the Jewish Communities of Morocco, 1862–1962. Albany: State University of New York Press, 1983.
Lattes, Guglielmo.
Vita e opere di Elia Benamozegh: Cenni, Considerazioni, Notes con Ritratto dell' Illustre Rabbino. Livorno: Stab. Tip. S. Belforte e.c., 1901.

Lebel, Jennie.
"'Lovesick for Jerusalem' — Rabbi Yehuda Alkalai, the Political and Communal Context of His Activity," *Pe'amim* 40 (1989) [Hebrew].
Lewis, Bernard.
The Shaping of the Modern Middle East. New York and Oxford: Oxford University Press, 1994.
Lyotard, Jean-François.
The Post Modern Condition: A Report on Knowledge. Translated by Geoff Bennington and Brian Massumi. Minneapolis: University of Minnesota Press, 1989.
Makariyus, Shahin.
Ta'rikh al-Isra'iliyyin. Cairo: Maṭbaʿat al-Muqtaṭaf, 1904.
Mayers, Michael A.
Response to Modernity: A History of the Reform Movement in Judaism. New York and Oxford: Oxford University Press, 1988.
Morgenstern, Arie.
"Between Rabbi Yehuda Bibas and an Emissary of the Perushim in Jerusalem," *Pe'amim* 40 (1989) [Hebrew].
Nini, Yehuda.
Mi-Mizraḥ umi-Yam: Yehude Miṣrayim, Ḥayye Yom Yom ve-Hishtaqfutam be-Sifrut ha-Shut, 5642–5674. Tel Aviv: Tel Aviv University, 1979/80.
Ovadia, David.
La Communauté de Sefrou. Vol. 3. Jerusalem: Makhon le-Ḥeqer Toldot Qehillot Yehude Maroqo, 1975.
Peres, Yochanan.
Ethnic Relations in Israel. 2nd ed. Tel Aviv: Sifriat Poʿalim and Tel Aviv University, 1977 [Hebrew].
Reinharz, Jehuda.
Fatherland or Promised Land: The Dilemma of the German Jew, 1893–1914. Ann Arbor: University of Michigan Press, 1975.
Roth, Cecil.
The House of Nasi: The Duke of Naxos. Philadelphia: Jewish Publication Society, 1948.
Sawicki, Tom.
"Inside the World of Mystic Healers," *The Jerusalem Report* (January 27, 1994).
Schechtman, Joseph B.
On Wings of Eagles: The Plight, Exodus, and Homecoming of Oriental Jewry. New York and London: Thomas Yoseloff, 1961.
Shochat, Azriel.
Beginnings of the Haskalah among German Jewry. Jerusalem: Bialik Institute, 1960 [Hebrew].
Shokeid, Moshe.
"Cultural Ethnicity in Israel: The Case of Middle Eastern Jews' Religiosity," *AJS Review* 9 (1984).
and Shlomo Deshen. *Distant Relations: Ethnicity and Politics among Arabs and North African Jews in Israel*. New York: Praeger, 1982.
The Predicament of Homecoming: Cultural and Social Life of North African Immigrants in Israel. Ithaca and London: Cornell University Press, 1974.

The Generation of Transition: Continuity and Change Among North African Immigrants in Israel. Jerusalem: Ben Zvi Institute, 1977 [Hebrew].

Shulewitz, M. H.

"Astruc, Jean," Encyclopaedia Judaica. Vol. 3.

Slouschz, Nahum.

Travels in North Africa. Philadelphia: Jewish Publication Society, 1927.

Smooha, Sammy.

Israel: Pluralism and Conflict. Berkeley and Los Angeles: University of California Press, 1978

and Don Peretz. "Israel's 1992 Knesset Elections: Are They Critical?" *Middle East Journal* 47 (Summer 1993).

Snoussi, Mohammad Larbi.

"Aux origines du movement sioniste en Tunisie à la veille de la grande guerre. Création de "l'Aghoudat Sion" et sa première scission (1887–1914)," *Les Cahiers de Tunisie* 44 (1991).

Sobel, Zvi and Benjamin Beit-Hallahmi, editors.

Tradition, Innovation, Conflict: Jewishness and Judaism in Contemporary Israel. Albany: State University of New York Press, 1991.

Somekh, ʿAbd Allah Abraham Joseph,

Zive Ṣedeq. Part 2. Jerusalem: Institut Bne Issakhar, 1986/87.

Shu"T Zivḥe Ṣedeq ha-Ḥadashot. Part 3. Jerusalem: Makhon Or ha Mizraḥ, 1981.

Stillman, Norman A.

"Fading Shadows of the Past: Jews in the Islamic World," in *Survey of Jewish Affairs 1989*. Edited by William Frankel. Oxford: Basil Blackwell Ltd., 1989.

The Jews of Arab Lands in Modern Times. Philadelphia: Jewish Publication Society, 1991.

"Moslems and Jews: The Connections Between the Mimouna Festival and Moslem Jewish Coexistence," *Jerusalem Post Supplement* (April 3, 1983).

Ta-Shma, Israel.

"Mekiẓe Nirdamim," *Encyclopaedia Judaica*. Vol. 11

Turner, Victor.

Dramas, Fields, and Metaphors: Symbolic Action in Human Society. Ithaca, New York: Cornell University Press, 1974.

Udovitch, Abraham L. and Lucette Valensi.

The Last Arab Jews: The Communities of Jerba, Tunisia. Chur, London, Paris, and New York: Harwood Academic Publishers, 1984.

Vital, David.

Origins of Zionism. Oxford: Clarendon Press, 1975.

Watt, William Montgomery.

Islamic Fundamentalism and Modernity. London and New York: Routledge, 1988.

Weingrod, Alex.

The Saint of Beersheba. Albany: State University of New York Press, 1990.

Yehuda, Zvi.

"Aliya from Iraq in the Early 1920s: Survey and Problematics," in *From Babylon to Jerusalem*. Tel Aviv: Iraqi Jews Traditional Culture Center, Institute for Research on Iraqi Jewry, 1980.

"The Place of Aliyah in Moroccan Jewry's Conception of Zionism," *Studies in Zionism* 6 (1985).

Organized Zionism in Morocco: 1900–1948. Unpublished doctoral dissertation, Jerusalem: Hebrew University, 1981. Vol. 1. [Hebrew].

Ydit, Meir.

"Ḥukkat ha-Goi," *Encyclopaedia Judaica*. Vol. 8.

Youssef, Michael.

Revolt Against Modernity: Muslim Zealots and the West. Leiden: E. J. Brill, 1985.

Zohar, Zvi.

Halakha u-Modernizaṣiyya: Darkhe He'anut Ḥakhme Miṣrayim le-Etgare ha-Modernizaṣiyya, 1822–1882. Jerusalem: Makhon Shalom Hartmann, 1982.

"The Halakhic Teaching of Egyptian Rabbis in Modern Times," *Pe'amim* 16 (1983) [Hebrew].

"The Attitude of Rabbi Abdallah Somekh towards Changes in the Nineteenth Century as Reflected in His Halakhic Writings," *Pe'amim* 36 (1988) [Hebrew].

Tradition and Change: Halakhic Responses of Middle Eastern Rabbis to Legal and Technological Change (Egypt and Syria, 1880–1920). Jerusalem: Ben Zvi Institute, 1993 [in Hebrew].

Index

science and technology 4, 13, 14, 16, 24, 26–28, 37, 38
secularism 7, 10, 11, 17, 21, 67, 69, 70
Sefrou 19
servi in camera 1
Sfax 60
sha`atnez 22
Shach, Eliezer 78
Shas Party 64, 78, 80, 84
She'erit ha-Naḥala 15
Shokeid, Moshe 67, 71, 74
Shulḥan `Arukh 43
Simeon Bar Yoai 74
Sofer, Moses (Ḥatam Sofer) 11, 24
Somekh, `Abd Allah 17, 24–26, 38
Spain 35, 65
Spanish language 29
Spinoza, Benedict 12
Sulayman the Magnificent 52
synagogues 14, 40, 41, 70, 71, 84, ethnic communal 71, 84
Syria 14, 20, 62

Ta`alumot Lev 45
ṭallit qaṭan 22
Tami Party 64
Tanzimat 13, 36
technology. *See* science and technology.
Tel Aviv 46, 71
Tetouan 16
Tiberias 53
Tiferet Yisra'el school 18
Torczyner, A. 60
Tripoli 21, 34, 36, 37
Tunisia(n) 18, 30, 37, 58, 60, 62, 63, 75
Turkey 29, 37, 54, 65
Turkish language 18, 19
Turner, Victor 74
Ṭuv Miṣrayim 45

ultra-Orthodoxy 3, 59, 77, 78, 84, 85
Umi-Ṣur Devash 45

Vital, David 50
Volozhin yeshiva 17

Weizmann, Chaim 62
Western Europe(an) 1, 56, 57, 60, 63
Western Sephardim 12
women 14, 39, 42, 53
World War I 13, 14, 60, 62, 63
World War II 6, 65
World Zionist Organization 6, 49, 63, 64

Yahadut ha-Torah ha-Me'uḥedet Party 78
Yehuda, Zvi 63
Yemen 69
yeshivas 16, 17, 54, 77, 78, 84, 85
Yiddish language and culture 2, 77
Yosef, Ovadia 78, 80, 81

Zikhron Yerushalayim 30, 33, 34, 44
Zionism (-ist) 2, 5–7, 34, 49–64, 66, 67, 69
Zohar 74
Zohar Zvi 38